And others

Church Unity

Five Lectures Delivered in the Union Theological Seminary, New York, during the

Winter of 1896

And others

Church Unity
Five Lectures Delivered in the Union Theological Seminary, New York, during the Winter cf 1896

ISBN/EAN: 9783337252410

Printed in Europe, USA, Canada, Australia, Japan

Cover: Foto ©Lupo / pixelio.de

More available books at **www.hansebooks.com**

CHURCH UNITY

Five Lectures

DELIVERED IN THE UNION THEOLOGICAL
SEMINARY, NEW YORK, DURING
THE WINTER OF 1896

BY

CHARLES W. SHIELDS, D.D., LL.D.
E. BENJAMIN ANDREWS, LL.D.
JOHN F. HURST, D.D., LL.D.
HENRY C. POTTER, D.D., LL.D.
AMORY H. BRADFORD, D.D.

NEW YORK
CHARLES SCRIBNER'S SONS
1896

Copyright, 1896,
BY CHARLES SCRIBNER'S SONS.

𝔘𝔫𝔦𝔳𝔢𝔯𝔰𝔦𝔱𝔶 𝔓𝔯𝔢𝔰𝔰:
JOHN WILSON AND SON, CAMBRIDGE, U.S.A.

PREFACE

THROUGH the kind provision of a Director of the Union Theological Seminary, five leading divines, representing five great evangelical churches, lectured in the Union Theological Seminary, during the winter of 1896, on the several topics of Church Unity assigned them. These lectures were so able, so timely, and so valuable, that it was deemed wise to publish them. They are printed just as delivered, with the exception of slight corrections and additions. The order was changed in a single instance, that the themes might be printed in a better chronological series. The lecturers were entirely free to express their own opinions upon the topics assigned them. Each author is exclusively responsible for his own lecture. The concord of opinion of these five representative divines with regard to Church Unity is quite remarkable. This concord expresses the spirit and attitude of the Union Theological Seminary.

CONTENTS

I

THE GENERAL PRINCIPLES OF CHURCH UNITY 3

By the Rev. CHARLES W. SHIELDS, D.D., LL.D., Professor in the College of New Jersey, Princeton, New Jersey.

II

THE SIN OF SCHISM 69

By the Rev. E. BENJAMIN ANDREWS, LL.D., President of Brown University, Providence, Rhode Island.

III

THE IRENIC MOVEMENTS SINCE THE REFORMATION 107

By the Rev. JOHN F. HURST, D.D., LL.D., Bishop of the Methodist Episcopal Church, Washington, D.C.

IV

	PAGE
THE CHICAGO-LAMBETH ARTICLES . . .	157

By the Right Rev. HENRY C. POTTER, D.D., LL.D., Bishop of New York.

V

THE UNITY OF THE SPIRIT — A WORLD-WIDE NECESSITY 199

By the Rev. AMORY H. BRADFORD, D.D., Pastor of Congregational Church, Montclair, New Jersey.

I

THE GENERAL PRINCIPLES OF CHURCH UNITY

By the Rev. CHARLES W. SHIELDS, D.D., LL.D.
*Professor in the College of New Jersey,
Princeton, New Jersey*

THE GENERAL PRINCIPLES OF CHURCH UNITY

THE cause of Church Unity still lives. Some of our denominational journals may seem to have been burying it with military honors, — But burying it only in effigy. It rises again before us, not as a spectre from the grave, but as the queen of the heavenly graces, with a train of reverend and learned advocates. It has long had its enthusiastic friends who were discreetly praised as amiable visionaries; now, apparently, it has some alarmed foes, who have betrayed no languid interest in the "iridescent dreamers." And so it takes its place among the living issues of the day.

THE CHURCH UNITY MOVEMENT

Is any issue more living? He must be blind indeed who does not see that the movement for church unity has become the characteristic movement of modern Christendom. Other questions, matters of doctrine or policy, may agitate certain portions of the Church here and there; but this is the one question which moves the whole Church everywhere, in both hemispheres. There is no corner of the Christian world, no outpost of Christian missions, to which it has not penetrated; and no grade of the Christian ministry, from the Pope himself down to the humblest evangelist, that has not voiced its claims. The Roman Church has been proposing terms of unity to the Greek Church, on the one hand, and to the Anglican Church on the other; the Anglican Church has been proposing terms to the other reformed churches; and all churches in the United States have been proposing terms to one another. Not only have kindred churches, long estranged, been reuniting, — Congregational with Congregational, Presbyterian with Presbyterian, Episcopal with Episcopal; not only have groups of such churches been forming international alliances, — Pan-Anglican, Pan-Presbyterian, Pan-Congregationalist, Pan-Methodist; but ready champions of such groups of churches, in truly ecumenical conferences, as at Cologne, Bonn, and Grünwald, have been approaching the problem of unity from the most diverse positions. Meanwhile, too, the great Christian heart of the age has been praying and hoping, as never before, that Christ's own prayer for oneness might be fulfilled.

EXPLANATIONS OF THE MOVEMENT

A movement so universal and deep-seated as this cannot be regarded as any mere accidental outburst or religious fashion of the time. The student of church history sees in it only an age-spirit which has been born of the ages. It appears to him in this light from various points of view. According to one view, ingenious but fanciful, the trend toward unity is but the issue of great Christian tendencies which from the first were typified by the three chief apostles as their representatives. The legal spirit of Peter and the evangelical spirit of Paul are to be harmonized by the loving spirit of John. As in the early Church the Petrine type of Jewish Christianity was opposed by the

Pauline type of Gentile Christianity, so in the later Church Catholicism has followed St. Peter until it denied his Lord in the papacy; while Protestantism, like St. Paul, has blamed and withstood it until freedom has become license. And now in the modern Church, Protestantism and Catholicism are to be reconciled under the gentle spirit of St. John, the beloved apostle, still tarrying till his Lord shall come. The reunited Church, like the bride in the Apocalypse, will then be prepared and adorned for her husband.

According to another and profounder view, the problem of church unity has simply come last in the logical evolution of Christian doctrine. To each age of Christianity has been given its own problems, to be solved and then left as premises to succeeding ages. The age of the Greek fathers was occupied with the problems of theology, strictly so called, and settled for all time the doctrines of the trinity, creation and incarnation. The next following age of the Latin fathers was devoted to the problems of anthropology, and defined the doctrines of original sin, electing grace, regeneration. Then came the age of the reformers, with the problems of soteriology, and new dogmatic definitions of the atonement, justification, and sanctification. At last we have reached an age of irenic thought, which must take up the problems of ecclesiology and discuss the doctrines of the Church, the ministry, and the sacraments. In the settlement of such questions the unity of the Church, as based upon a doctrinal consensus of the Christian ages, would appear as that last problem of problems, by the solution of which the circle of Christian doctrine is to be completed.

According to another and more philosophical view, the present impulse to church unity is but a natural and healthy reaction from former impulses to church division. It illustrates that great historic law of recurrences, by which whole generations after having been driven toward one extreme will rebound toward the other, until they settle down to a just medium. For some centuries past the divisive impulse has been working with frightful momentum. In the ninth century the Western Church broke away from the Eastern

Church. In the sixteenth century the reformed Churches broke away from the Roman church; and for three centuries since then they have gone on reforming the Reformation, protesting against Protestantism, purifying Puritanism, dissenting from dissent, dividing, redividing and sub-dividing down to the inorganic dust of individuality itself. The absurd result has been reached that every Christian man may do without the Church, or any chance meeting of Christian men may manufacture the Church anew, in ignorance of all the Christian centuries before them and in contempt of all Christendom around them. At length, however, from these wild extremes the inevitable reaction has set in during the present century, at first faint and feeble but gathering strength and volume in its course. The general recoil of modern towards primitive Christianity has been followed by that of Protestantism toward Catholicity, Puritanism towards Ecclesiasticism, dissent towards consent. American Christianity, hitherto so unhistoric, is beginning to see that something is due to the wisdom of the Christian ages and the consent of Christian nations. As different thinkers variously express it, "the centrifugal age of Christianity is closed; The centripetal action has begun."[1] "The age of division is over: that of reunion is coming on." Thus viewed, the movement for church unity is but a recoil from the sectarian results of the Reformation under the great historic law of action and reaction, cause and effect.

Still another and the most practical view is, that the unification of the Church has become necessary by its critical position in modern civilization. Christianity has ever been more or less involved in the civilization which has accompanied it as part of its own historic development. In the primitive age it encountered a Pagan civilization, whose art, philosophy, and politic were hostile to its lofty claims. In the middle ages, it had Christianized and conquered this pagan civilization, rendering its philosophy a handmaid to divinity, resolving its art into a stately ritual, and subjecting even the State to the Church. But now, in the present reforming age, it finds itself divorced, falsely and tempo-

[1] Rev. Prof. George P. Fisher, DD.

rarily, from the very civilization to which it has itself given birth; surrounded by a sceptical philosophy, a licentious art, and a politic wholly of the earth earthy. Not only thus surrounded by agnosticism, immorality, anarchism; but internally rent and torn with sectarianism, rationalism, formalism. Never before was there such need of an organic consolidation of the conservative forces of Chistianity. Never before was there such need of an organic compact of its aggressive forces. Never before was there such need of presenting a united Church to heathenism abroad and to irreligion at home. In this light unity appears simply indispensable to the Church to enable it to accomplish its final earthly mission as a teacher, conservator, and regenerator of human society.

These are some explanations of the unity movement. There is truth in each of them. All of them may be combined consistently. We may view the movement as at once a reconciliation of Christian temperaments, a completion of Christian doctrine, a reaction from the sectarian results of the Reformation, and a necessity of Chistian civilization; or we may attempt no explanation, and accept it simply as an inscrutable Providence, — the fact remains, that it is the supreme question of our Christian epoch.

Before discussing the general principles of Church unity, we need to define the sense in which the words are to be used. It is not now proposed to speak of the Church as invisible and unorganized; nor of a unity that is sentimental and ideal; but of the visible organized Church and of a visible organic unity. Never, indeed, should we forget or depreciate that glorious invisible Church or communion of saints which includes all true believers in Christ that are, or have been, or shall be united to Him, whether in heaven or upon earth. Much less may we set forth as opposed or superior to the one invisible Church that other visible Church which is now so divided, distracted, and even dismembered. Rather must we discern a fixed normal relation of the one to the other, and ever aim, as far as in us lies, to make the visible Church a true expression of the invisible Church, in its unity as well as in its other divine qualities. This view of church unity as organic may be vindicated on several grounds.

ORGANIC UNITY INTENDED BY OUR LORD

In the first place, organic unity was contemplated by our Lord himself as head of the Church. Although he was pre-eminently a teacher, he was also an organizer. He instituted a church as well as proclaimed a gospel. And he gave to that church apostles, sacraments, scriptures, doctrines, all of which are strictly ecclesiastical elements, appertaining only to a Church visible. As far as was practicable during his own lifetime, he thus organized his spiritual kingdom; and after ascending into heaven he completed the organization, by conferring upon it apostles, prophets, evangelists, pastors, and doctors, for the edifying of his body in the unity of his faith and of his knowledge. This was the one visible Church as organized by Christ himself; and it is inconceivable, that he ever intended it should be broken into jarring sects, calling themselves His Church, excommunicating one another, denying each other's ministry and sacraments and having no more inter-communion than the Jews and Samaritans. To imagine Him, in his last great intercession on the night of his betrayal, praying for a mere invisible unity as consistent with visible schism and conflict, would make that solemn utterance either a truism or an absurdity. Most distinctly He prayed, not only that the oneness of all believers might be as essential as that between the Father and himself, but that it might be manifested as demonstrative proof of his earthly mission, — "that the world may know that thou hast sent me." And not until all sectarianism has disappeared from His visible organized Church will the prayer be fulfilled.

ORGANIC UNITY TAUGHT BY THE APOSTLES

In the second place, organic unity was also inculcated by the apostles as founders of the Church. By their official acts they proceeded to give it the ecclesiastical equipment of ministry, sacrament, scripture, and doctrine, and in their Epistles they ever rebuked divisions as schisms and magnified organic unity as essential in the visible Church of Christ. Ecclesiastical diversities, much less extreme than those now known as Congregationalist, Presbyterian, and Episcopalian, were characterized as the wildest hallucination, a mere delirious dream of the members of a diseased body saying one to another, "I have no need of thee." Doctrinal distinctions, made by teachers much less known than Luther, Calvin, or Wesley, met with the stern rebuke, "Is Christ divided? Were ye baptised into the name of Paul?" Ritual usages, much more menacing than those which now separate Baptist and Pedobaptist, Evangelist and Sacerdotalist, were settled by the apostles and elders in the first Council of Jerusalem without the unchristian results of schism and sectarianism. And this organic unity of the Apostolic Church was maintained unbroken for centuries afterwards, — at least until the Council of Nice.

ORGANIC UNITY MAINTAINED BY THE REFORMERS

In the third place, this organic unity was never repudiated by the Protestants or Reformers of later time. As those words imply, had it been possible, they would have remained in the Roman Church, simply protesting against its errors and reforming its abuses. They had no thought of destroying Catholic unity. Luther distinguished between Popery and that true ancient Roman Church of the early fathers, from which he never considered himself separated. Melanchthon even injured his fame by his efforts to retain Lutheranism under the papacy and in harmony with Calvinism. Calvin not only claimed agreement with the true ancient Church of Chrysostom and Basil, of Cyprian, Ambrose, and Augustine; but formulated a consensus of the reformed churches; and when Archbishop Cranmer proposed a general council for defining the principles of Church unity, declared he would have crossed ten seas rather than miss that Lambeth Conference. Moreover, during the first century after the Reformation all the reformed churches, including the Church of England, sat together in the same synods, interchanged pulpits and professors' chairs, and recognized the validity of each others' ministry and sacraments. It would seem inconsistent with historic truth and good scholarship for their American descendants now to call any of these branches of the Catholic Church "sects" or "schisms," however fitly the terms may be applied to some Christian bodies of later date. In law and courtesy they are entitled "churches," as in the preface of the Prayer-book; and we shall never get before us all the data of the Church unity problem until we have studied afresh the organic connection of the Evangelical Lutheran Church, the Reformed Dutch and German Church, the Protestant Episcopal Church, and the Presbyterian Church, with the whole visible Catholic Church of Christ and his apostles.

ORGANIC UNITY ATTAINABLE

In the fourth place, such organic unity is the only kind of Church unity which is practicable or directly attainable by our efforts. The invisible Church unity, of which we have spoken, is a divinely constituted relationship of believers in Christ, which we can neither create nor destroy, but only express and maintain. Seen by the eye of God alone, but for the visible Church such unity would be to us invisible indeed. In this world, at least, there could be no communion of saints without ecclesiastical organization. The unity of the spirit would be a mere sentiment or notion, if even conceivable. It is in the sphere of organic unity that our duty and privilege lie. And there we may attempt little or much. Indeed, we shall attempt nothing at all if we simply accept the present condition of the visible Church as normal, necessary, and perpetual. We shall only continue to exhibit the mystical body of Christ to the world as seemingly mutilated or deliriously dismembered. Nor shall we attempt very much more, if we are content to give the invisible unity, our common Christian oneness, merely some faint and transient expression, as in united missions, united charities, evangelical alliances, and denominational leagues and federations for social, civic, and national reform. Too much cannot be said in praise of such Christian associations, when viewed as to their own beneficent aims and results. But after all that may be said, it still remains to be said, it is not their distinctive mission to promote church unity. They may even obscure and thwart such unity, if put in place of Scripture ideals and precepts and allowed to exhaust the Christian instinct and effort toward oneness.

Speaking now simply to the point, I have little faith in any occasional schemes or forms of Christian union which do not both aim and tend to become organic, ecclesiastical, historic, apostolical, and scriptural. Nor do I find myself turned from this view by the popular objections which we hear on all sides: "Denominationalism is itself a great blessing;" "Christians will have to become much better than they are now;" "Church unity is a thing of the millennium." On the contrary, as I have tried to show on former occasions, all that is good in denominationalism would be consistent with a true church unity, and without it simply tends to sectarianism. With all their faults, the Christians of our day, as Christians go in this evil world, are no worse than those who have gone before us or are likely to come after us. Nor have we a right to devolve our duty upon an unknown posterity in the millennium, whenever that may come. The true chasers of the rainbow are those strict denominationalists who would paint upon the dark cloud of our unhappy divisions the "iridescent dream" of some ideal church of the future, which is so remote and vague that we can never reach it until we have all become transfigured into saints and angels. If we will only begin with Christians as they are and churches and denominations as we find them, and inquire how to render them one united Church, we shall at least be dealing with the facts of the situation.

It follows now from these definitions that the principles of church unity must consist of fixed ecclesiastical tenets and institutes rather than mere abstract propositions, sentimental professions, or occasional co-operations. As yet, the only scheme of such principles which has entered the field and still keeps the field, is known as the Quadrilateral, or Four Lambeth Principles. A word is needed as to its history.

HISTORY OF THE QUADRILATERAL

To the Protestant Episcopal Church belongs the honor — an honor which can never be taken away from her — of having first enunciated in our day any general principles of church unity. Perhaps it was but natural and right that the rallying call should come from a denomination so churchly in its aim and spirit and so fitted by its historic antecedents to lead the other American denominations toward Catholicity. Certain it is that within this communion, almost from its origin, the question has been under lively discussion. The patriarchal Bishop White, after the Revolution, not only gave the Episcopalian body a Presbyterian constitution of the vertebrate type, but also favored organic connection with the Moravian, Methodist, and Lutheran communions. The prophetical Bishop Seabury, at the same time, though he founded a different school of churchmanship, named as the four fixed marks of the Church, — government, sacrament, faith, and doctrine, which are very suggestive of the Lambeth postulates.[1] But it was reserved for the saintly and beloved Muhlenberg, combining both schools in himself as "an Evangelical Catholic," to give the whole movement voice and potency. In the famous Memorial of 1853, composed by him and addressed to the bishops, the

---

[1] History of the Prot. Episc. Church, by Archdeacon Charles C. Tiffany, DD., p. 557, 562.

query was raised, whether the Protestant Episcopal Church, with only her present canonical means and appliances, her fixed and invariable modes of worship, and her traditional customs and usages, is competent to the work of preaching and dispensing the gospel to all sorts and conditions of men in this land and in this age: and whether her mission might not be more fully accomplished by the extension of Episcopal ordination to "men in other Christian bodies, who would gladly receive it could they obtain it without that entire surrender of all the liberty in public worship to which they have been accustomed, — men who are sound in the faith and having the gift of preachers and pastors would be able ministers of the New Testament." It was further urged by the Memorialists, that to the Catholic episcopate belongs the high privilege of becoming the central bond of church unity in Protestant Christendom, and that it may be the special work of an American episcopate to attempt some "broader and more comprehensive ecclesiastical system, surrounding and including the Protestant Episcopal Church as it is now, leaving that church untouched, identical with that church in all its great principles, yet providing for as much freedom in opinion, discipline, and worship as is compatible with the essential faith and order of the Gospel." This noble project was so novel and startling at that time, forty years ago, that it does not seem even to have been fully comprehended. Its temporary failure was followed, as might have been foreseen, by the rise of the ritualistic party and the secession of the Reformed Episcopal Church. But its good effects have remained in the appointment of a permanent Episcopal Commission on Church Unity, in a revision of the Prayer-Book, enriching it and making it more flexible, and in the Declaration concerning Unity by the General Convention of 1886, at Chicago.

THE CHICAGO ARTICLES OF UNITY

The Chicago Declaration was issued in response to a memorial signed by more than eleven hundred clergymen, including thirty-two bishops, and by over three thousand laymen. It is understood to have been elaborated in purport and language by Bishop Littlejohn, of Long Island, chairman of the Episcopal Commission.[1] In the preamble, after referring to the Muhlenberg Memorial, the bishops declared: (1) their earnest desire that the Saviour's prayer for unity may be speedily fulfilled; (2) their belief that all duly baptised persons are members of the Holy Catholic Church; (3) their readiness to forego all things of mere human ordering as to modes of worship and discipline or traditional customs; and (4) their disavowal of any wish to absorb other Christian communions into their own church, but only to co-operate with such communions on the basis of a common faith and order, to discountenance schism and heal the wounds in the body of Christ. At the same time, the bishops affirm, that the unity sought can only be obtained by a return of all Christian communions to its first principles as exemplified by the primitive, undivided

---

[1] The Rev. Dr. Huntington, of Grace Church, in his "Essay towards Unity," also foreshadowed some of its essential statements, and gave to the four articles the name of "Quadrilateral," by which they have become known. "These four points, like the four famous fortresses of Lombardy, make the 'Quadrilateral' of pure Anglicanism." — p. 157.

Church, and entrusted as a sacred deposit of faith and order by Christ and his apostles to the Church through all time, and therefore as incapable of compromise or surrender by those who have been ordained to be its stewards and trustees for the common and equal benefit of all men. And then the bishops set forth four such principles of church unity.

First. The Holy Scriptures, as the revealed word of God.

Second. The Nicene Creed, as the essential faith.

Third. The two Sacraments, as instituted by Christ.

Fourth. The Historic Episcopate, as locally adapted to different Christian nations.

The bishops concluded with an expression of their readiness for brotherly conference with any Christian bodies seeking the restoration of the organic unity of the Church with a view to the earnest study of the conditions under which so priceless a blessing might happily be brought to pass. This is substantially the whole purport of the Chicago Declaration.

THE LAMBETH ARTICLES OF UNITY

The next stage in the history is to be traced in the proceedings of the last Pan-Anglican Conference, convened by the Archbishop of Canterbury at Lambeth Palace in 1888. It appears that for more than thirty years a movement like that on this side of the ocean had been gaining strength and clearness in the convocations both of Canterbury and York, as well as in the colonial synods of Canada and Australia; and by the time it came before the assembled bishops it had pervaded the whole Anglican communion throughout the world. The result of their deliberations was the adoption of the four American articles with two slight amendments. In the first article the Holy Scriptures are not characterized simply "as the revealed Word of God," but more precisely "as containing all things necessary to salvation and as being the rule and ultimate standard of faith." In the second article "the Apostles' Creed, as the baptismal symbol," was added to "the Nicene Creed, as the sufficient statement of the Christian faith." There were, however, some significant changes in the preamble and supplement of the American Declaration. The entire preamble was omitted. Consequently, the Four Principles are no longer offered to other communions " as inherent parts of a sacred deposit of faith and order incapable of compromise or surrender by those who have been ordained to be its stewards and trustees." To some persons this may seem a very important omission. For one, I do not think much would be gained or lost to either party by retaining it. But inasmuch as the prelatic claim of trusteeship is not generally admitted, it may be well to have the terms of unity as much freed from debatable matter as possible. In place of the discarded preamble, the Quadrilateral is presented simply as supplying " a basis on which approach may be by God's blessing made toward Home-reunion " — a phrase explained elsewhere as affording "a basis for a United Church, including at least the chief Christian communions of our people," — " with large freedom of variation on secondary points of doctrine, worship, and discipline." [1]

The supplement of the American Decla-

[1] Lambeth Conferences of 1888, pp. 280, 333–335.

ration was also modified. Instead of referring to other churches somewhat vaguely as "Christian bodies," the Conference definitely characterizes them as having "standards of doctrine, worship, and government;" expresses the belief that "even in respect of Church government" a basis of agreement may be found with non-conforming communions; announces a readiness for brotherly conference with them, "in order to consider what steps can be taken, either toward corporate reunion, or toward such relations as may prepare the way for fuller organic unity hereafter;" and finally, with a view to this end, recommends a comparative study of "the standards of the Anglican Church and the authoritative standards of doctrine, worship, and government adopted by the other bodies into which the English-speaking races are divided."[1]

It will be seen that the logical effect of the Pan-Anglican revision has been to detach the Lambeth principles, as they may now be called,[2] from local and denomina-

[1] Lambeth Conferences, p. 281.
[2] The Convention at Baltimore adopted formally the Four Principles as amended by the Lambeth Conference.

national peculiarities in both the American and Anglican churches, and to plant them in the midst of all English-speaking communions as tenets of Catholic unity. There they stand to-day. They may be deserted by those who planted them there, and be left as a monumental folly on the highway of time; or they may become henceforth the rallying standard of a reunited Christendom.

Without attempting a full exposition of these principles, we need only in this lecture take a general view of their fitness to the ecclesiastical situation in our own country. They may be regarded as affording a consensus of Catholic churches; of Protestant churches; of Protestant with Catholic churches.

THE LAMBETH CONSENSUS OF CATHOLIC CHURCHES.

And first let us consider their fitness to those great historic churches, the Orthodox Greek and Roman Catholic, which though they have their seat in Europe, extend their jurisdiction over portions of the American people. The Greek Church, numbering some eighty-four millions in

Christendom, prevails as yet only in the territory of Alaska, with a few scattered congregations in our cities; but religious or political events may yet give it more American importance. It possesses all the Four Lambeth Principles, encumbered by dogmas and rites more or less inconsistent with them. It holds the first article, while adding the authority of tradition to that of Scripture. It holds the second article, while rejecting from the Nicene Creed the clause which teaches the double procession of the Holy Spirit from the Father *and the Son* (*Filioque*). It holds the third article, but adds to the two sacraments of our Lord the church sacraments of confirmation, penance, holy orders, extreme unction, and matrimony; administers baptism and the eucharist to mere infants, with trine immersion and presbyterial confirmation; and includes in its ritual the intercession of saints, the adoration of the Virgin, and the worship of sacred pictures. It holds the fourth article, though superimposing upon the historic episcopate a patriarchate which at times has rivalled the papacy. The Roman Catholic Church, numbering two hundred and fifteen millions of Christians, with at least eight millions in the United States, has been growing enormously by natural increase and immigration. It also maintains the Four Principles, but in connection with even more serious inconsistencies. To Holy Scripture it has added, not only apostolic tradition, but a papal infallibility in interpreting both Scripture and tradition. To the Nicene Creed it has added not only the *Filioque*, by which it excommunicated all Eastern Christendom, but the dogmas of Trent, by which it excommunicated the whole Protestant body. To the two sacraments it has added not only the five other church sacraments not instituted by Christ, but the doctrine of transubstantiation, the denial of the cup, masses for souls in purgatory, the invocation of saints, the worship of relics, and a Mariolatry crowned with the dogma of the immaculate conception. And to the historic episcopate it has added not merely the Roman primacy, but the claims of a universal bishop and vicar of Christ on earth. It is plain, that the discord of Anglican with Greek and Latin Christianity is far greater than the concord.

THE LAMBETH CONSENSUS OF PROTESTANT CHURCHES.

As we pass to the Protestant side of Christendom we find the picture reversed. The churches of the Reformation are largely in accord with the Lambeth articles. At the head is the Lutheran Church, with twenty million members in Europe and a million in America. It has retained the Holy Scriptures as the only rule of faith; the two creeds, together with the Athanasian Creed and the Augsburg Confession; the two sacraments, with large portions of the Catholic sacramentary; and the historic episcopate as an expedient institution in Germany, with an apostolical succession in Sweden and Moravia which is as undisputed as the Anglican and with which the American Lutheran communion is about to reinforce its evangelical ministry. Next appear the reformed churches, Dutch, French, and German, — less numerous but more potent as yet in our American Christianity. These churches retained the Scriptures as the very word of God written; the Apostles' Creed, with the Heidelberg Catechism and the Canons of Dort; and the two Sacraments, with General Confession and Absolution, and a simple Protestant liturgy. But being precluded by their political circumstances from reforming the historic episcopate, they continued the historic presbyterate, enriching it with those principles of lay representation and church freedom which have since passed into the Scottish and American churches. Then comes into view the Church of England, the most numerous and powerful of the English-speaking communions, though hitherto least potent in moulding our Christian institutions. The English Church in its reformation retained the canonical Scriptures as containing all things necessary to salvation; the two creeds, with the Athanasian Creed and the Thirty-nine Articles; the two sacraments, with a mixture of Catholic and Protestant formularies in its liturgy, with portions of the Roman Breviary in its daily service, and with the ceremonies of confirmation, matrimony, and burial in its ritual. But its historic episcopate being in the hands of baronial bishops, it naturally continued them as a prelatic order in the ministry, to which has since been easily attached the claim of an exclusive prelatic succession from the apostles. The corresponding American Church has acquired this Anglican episcopate as supported by an admirable Presbyterian house of deputies. Next we have the Church of Scotland, less beautiful than her queenly sister of England, but of the same lineage and the most vigorous ecclesiastical force in our Christian civilization. The Scottish Church also retained the canonical Scriptures; the Apostles' Creed, with the Westminster Confession as an expansion of the Thirty-nine Articles; and the two Sacraments connected with a Directory ensuring the unfailing use of the appointed words and elements; its Presbyterian associates in England having failed to establish the revised Prayer-Book. But, being less entangled with the old political hierarchy, it declared that it had been "reformed from popery, not by prelates, but by presbyters, as the only successors left by Christ and his apostles in the Church." And this historic presbyterate, as not inconsistent with the pure historic episcopate, but antedating both the prelatic and the papal sway in Britain, and confessedly traceable back to the apostles' time, has been perpetuated by the American presbyteries with scrupulous care through all their conflicts and separations. As to the strictly post-reformation communions, such as the Congregationalist, Baptist, and Methodist churches, so dominant in our evangelical Christianity, it need only be said that, although they do not formally profess the Lambeth principles, yet they are practically agreed in the first two articles; might find a consensus in the sacramental article by mutual tolerance; and could have their congregational, presbyterial, and episcopal elements normally combined in the historic episcopate, as in the undivided Apostolic Church, without loss of principle or prestige. In a word, when thus harmonized, the concord of Anglican with Protestant Christianity almost drowns the discord.

PROTESTANT AND CATHOLIC REUNION

In order to complete this survey let us now imagine Catholicism to have been reunited, and Protestantism to have been reunited, each on the Lambeth basis. The problem would then remain, to reunite Protestantism with Catholicism on the same basis. The elements of the problem are very mixed, — some favorable, some unfavorable. First among the former is the actual consent of the two sections of Christendom in the Lambeth principles. They already have at least one common rule of faith, much common catholic doctrine, two common sacraments, and a common historic ministry, whether traced from the apostles through pope, prelate, or presbyter. And from both sides some approaches have even been made toward reunion upon the basis of such a consensus. On the Catholic side we have had the official correspondence between the Anglican and Greek churches, through the Archbishop of Canterbury and the Patriarch of Constantinople; the Old Catholic Reformation from within the Roman Church protesting against the papal infallibility, and along other lines approximating Protestantism; the Bonn conferences looking to a confederation of Anglican, Russian, Greek, and Old Catholic churches on the basis of a primitive consensus existing before the division of Christendom and largely identical with the Lambeth principles; and finally, the

Encyclical Letters of the Roman Pontiff, inviting all Protestants and Orthodox Greek Christians to return to the Mother of churches.

PROTESTANT APPROACHES TOWARD REUNION

On the other side, we have no less remarkable approaches toward reunion, — such as the Catholic revival of the last fifty years in the Church of England, and more recently in the Church of Scotland; the general Protestant reaction, as shown in all denominations by a growing observance of the church year, a recovery of portions of the Catholic liturgy, and a renewed appreciation of church history and Christian antiquity. We have also an increasing association of Protestants with Catholics in many humanitarian and Christian movements. When it is added that in our own country the two have been brought under social fusion within a democratic environment, already engendering a Catholic type of Christianity in Protestantism, and a Protestant type of intelligence and freedom in Catholicism, the dream of reunion will not seem purely chimerical. Influenced by the glowing vision, a great scholar even imagined the Pope inviting "a fraternal Pan-Christian Council in Jerusalem, where the Mother Church of Christendom held the first council of reconciliation and peace. But," he adds, "whether in Jerusalem or Rome, or (as Cardinal Wiseman thought) in Berlin, or (as some Americans think) on the banks of the Mississippi, the war between Rome, Wittenberg, Geneva, and Oxford will be fought out to a peaceful end, when all the churches shall be throughly Christianized and all the creeds of Christendom unified in the creed of Christ."[1]

THE PROBLEM OF REUNION DIFFICULT

The problem, however, has other elements which are not so bright and hopeful, and may for the present turn the scale. It cannot be forgotten that the consensus of Protestant and Catholic opinion is not only greatly outweighed by the dissensus, but as yet is purely theoretical, having been expressed only in courteous correspondence without much substantial in-

[1] Dr. Schaff's "Reunion of Christendom," p. 28.

tercommunion. The Greek Church has never repealed the decrees of Constantinople against the Reformers. To some critics the occasional Anglican advances toward the Greek Church look like mere ecclesiastical coquetry or an adroit flank movement against the Roman Church, rather than direct attempts at true unity. The thirteen Patriarchs in their recent Encyclical have also repelled the papal advances. The Old Catholic movement was an external, not an internal, reformation of the Church of Rome, and was a mere ripple compared with the Eastern schism or the Protestant revolt. The Roman Catholic Church still stands, separated by the chasm of a thousand years from the Eastern Church, and by four centuries from all the Reformed churches, meanwhile having gained more in numbers than it had lost; and so far from relaxing the excommunicating decrees of Trent, has reinforced them with new dogmas, binding together its whole communion as with tenfold bands of steel. At the present moment it is demonstrating its prestige through a plenipotentiary delegate in the midst of our churches.

From the Protestant side, also, the approaches have been of a mixed issue, divisive as well as conciliatory. The Anglo-Catholic revival, however just and beautiful in itself, has thus far bred a harvest of reverts to Romanism, and is necessarily accompanied with an anti-papal policy not conducive to reunion. It is a jarring note even in the Chicago and Lambeth declarations. The Protestant reaction in other reformed churches, though inevitable and wise, is still overcharged with hatred of popery, and even meets the most patriotic advances with fresh outbursts of native Americanism. He must shut his eyes to facts who looks for a new Protestant Catholicism to be reached at a bound, as by a feat of logic or stroke of policy. That distant goal can only be approached with slow and painful steps, through alternate defeat and victory, as a conquered peace of the Church.

PROTESTANT UNIFICATION A PRE-REQUISITE

My design in thus stating this great problem has not been to indulge in mere prophetic visions, whether cheerful or gloomy, but rather to open the way for two important inferences from the whole survey, for which we are now ready. I can only state them without fully developing them. One of them is, that the ecclesiastical unification of Protestant Christianity on the Lambeth basis must precede the general reunion of Christendom. At least, for Anglo-Saxon Christians this is the first step and condition precedent. The Greek Church is still unreformed and overgrown with accumulated errors. The Latin Church, even more erroneous, is not only unreformed, but hostile. To indulge in wasteful attempts at unification with such communions is to begin at the end. We shall more wisely begin at the beginning, if we first seek unity where it is most needed and most hopefully pursued, in our own country and among our own divided churches and denominations. In combining them organically by means of the four ecclesiastical principles of a common rule of faith, a common creed, common sacraments, and a common ministry everywhere to be recognized as legitimate, we shall heal the sectarian diseases of Protestantism and repair the destructive effects of the Reformation. We shall secure at once a sounder Protestantism and a more constructive reformation, and so recover all that is best in Catholic Christianity while retaining all that is best in Protestant culture. And then, too, we shall have the vantage ground for influencing the older communions; in no hostile manner, but externally, by surrounding them, especially in this country, with the organized Christian intelligence of the age; and internally, by combining with any fresh Protestantism and new reformation within their own pale. It is mainly, if not solely, by a reactionary influence of Protestantism upon Catholicism that the two can ever be prepared for mutual appreciation, on the basis of common ecclesiastical principles. In a word, the reunion of Anglo-Saxon Christianity is essential to its reunion with Latin and Greek Christianity.

THE PRESBYTERIAN AND EPISCOPAL CHURCHES

The other inference is, that in this work of Protestant unification the Presbyterian

Church stands next to the Protestant Episcopal Church, as together with it holding the key of the situation. In this country, at least, they are the two chief English-speaking communions, and have a common mission in promoting American church unity. If it be granted that the Episcopal Church seems destined to be the Church of the Reconciliation, mediating between the extreme wings of Christendom by its combined Catholic and Protestant formularies, yet it still needs the balancing influences represented by the Presbyterian Church, on the one side, to prevent it from careening as a mere feeder to the Roman communion, and on the other side to keep it in vital connection with the whole reformed communion. Its theoretical position will otherwise become practically untenable. If it be urged that it is the natural nucleus of church unity in our Anglo-American civilization, yet the two sister churches have had a common history in the mother country and still have correlate standards, ecclesiastical affinities, and common interests, which fit them to march together as the advanced column toward the United Church of the United States, drawing after them other churches and denominations.[1] In a word, as the general reunion of Christendom turns upon the reunion of Protestantism and Catholicism, so the reunion of Protestantism and Catholicism turns upon the reunion of presbytery and episcopacy.

THE RECENT ECCLESIASTICAL CONFERENCES

It is a striking proof of the common mission of the two churches that as yet they are the only two communions in Christendom which have met on the Lambeth basis for formal conferences. During the past six years they have been

---

[1] It may be added, that the situation is complicated by rival claimants, Protestant as well as Catholic. Not only do the Orthodox Greek and Roman Catholic branches of the historic episcopate co-exist with the Protestant Episcopal in our country; but we have also the Moravian and Reformed episcopates, and are likely soon to have a Lutheran episcopate, all claiming equal validity with the Anglican. Amid this confusion and conflict of denominational episcopates, the unification of the Presbyterian and Protestant Episcopal churches may be important in maintaining the ascendency of the Anglo-American type of ecclesiastical Christianity in our civilization.

negotiating through authorized representatives. It is true, and a pity 't is true, that these conferences have met with a temporary check and recoil. But no irreconcilable differences have been brought to light. Simply some mistakes have been made, which it is easy now to understand. With the utmost respect and deference, I beg to state them frankly. On the one side, it was a mistake when negotiating with the Protestant Episcopal Church alone, to make common cause with other less ecclesiastical denominations on the trivial side-issue of an indiscriminate exchange of pulpits. And the mistake was aggravated by putting this "doctrine of ministerial reciprocity" offensively in front of other and weightier questions upon which it depended and making it a seeming condition of any further conferences. On the other side, it was a mistake to meet that side-issue in a newspaper symposium with a peace-measure which was like Dr. Pusey's Eirenicon, "an olive branch discharged from a catapult." And afterwards, when the Presbyterian Committee had explained their unfortunate action and sent such a messenger of peace,[1] was it wise, if quite just or necessary, to terminate the suspended conferences?[2] Such mistakes are mere passing shadows upon the onward movement, and will do more good than harm if they help us to see the real misconceptions which still becloud the situation on both sides of the horizon. Let us deal with them faithfully and in the spirit of the most perfect Christian candor and patience.

PRESBYTERIAN MISCONCEPTIONS

And first, the Presbyterian misconceptions. One of them is a general misapprehension of the spirit and motive of the Lambeth proposals. It is often said that our Episcopal friends are "insincere,"

---

[1] The Rev. Dr. Joseph T. Smith: "The visit was made, not on the invitation of the Episcopal Commission, but by appointment of the Presbyterian Committee. And this appointment was, under the circumstances, an act of such marked magnanimity that it ought to be known." *The Churchman*, February, 1896.

[2] "Whether right or wrong," says Dr. Smith, "the Episcopal Commission regarded the action of the Assembly of 1893 as an abandonment of the negotiations on which we had thus far been engaged and as equivalent to the expression of a desire on its part that all negotiations between us should cease."

"arrogant," "offensive," in offering terms of unity to other historic churches that they will only characterize as "Christian bodies," "sects," and even "dissenters." Such fashions of speech, whatever may be thought of them, do not alter facts and things. The Church of England is regarded as no better than a sect by the oldest churches in Christendom; and the Episcopal Church in Scotland is treated as only a dissenting Christian body, whose prelates could not lawfully take precedence of a Presbyterian minister. The gracious Queen herself devoutly receives Presbyterian communion. In a country like ours, with no established religion, why withhold the civil title "Church" while conceding the polite use of the ecclesiastical title "Reverend"? Such slights to some minds are as irritating as the Roman Catholic repudiation of Anglican orders. Nevertheless, the simple fact that in the face of such inconsistencies and at the risk of sacrificing courtesy to principle, some Episcopalians do take high churchly ground against Presbyterian orders, shows the strength and honesty of their convictions. Does any one doubt that they do not feel keenly their isolation from their fellow Christians? Why, they have been discussing among themselves this matter of church unity for fifty years, while Presbyterians have not moved an inch toward them. After much misgiving they have offered grave concessions, upon which Presbyterians have only advanced with fresh demands and scruples. One feels almost ashamed to notice such objections, when he thinks of that apostle of the movement, the noble-hearted Muhlenberg, and now, alas! of its zealous martyr, the lamented Langdon, to say nothing of its still living advocates, who are showing us every day that the strictest churchmanship may consist with an earnest desire for church unity.

There is also a Presbyterian misconception of the scope of the historic episcopate. Because that much misrepresented institution is sometimes vindicated on extreme High Church ground, as involving an exclusively prelatical transmission of supernatural grace from the apostles, and because it is proffered for acceptance with all the claims and appliances of a priestly ritual, it is inferred that such is the only opinion or theory that can be attached to it and made congruous with it. In point of fact, however, as every student of church history knows, the greatest variety of opinions and theories have been connected with it and are now loyally supporting it.[1] For this reason, from a

[1] The Rev. Francis J. Hall, in his lecture before the Church Club of New York, has done me the honor to comment upon this view of the historic episcopate, and I am glad to find it supported by his reasoning. He shows conclusively, that the Protestant Episcopal Church "has not inserted her doctrine of the Ministry in the constitution of her general convention;" that "she has nowhere set forth her doctrine of the Ministry in connected order and detail in her formularies;" and that "she has not defined the doctrine of Apostolical Succession in set terms" (pp. 158-161). In other words, it is not a Church dogma set forth in the Church standards as an essential part of the Catholic faith, but is simply a pious opinion neither enjoined nor forbidden. As an opinion it is indeed now held in various forms and degrees by various schools of churchmen; but as a so-called Catholic doctrine it is not defined, or even named, in the creeds, articles, ordinal, or Prayer-Book. The mere occurrence of the vague phrase, "Ministers of the Apostolical Succession," in an American collect seldom used, is not a definition of Catholic doctrine; nor would that phrase, as strictly construed, imply anything more than a general or presbyterial succession of the whole Christian ministry.

As no view of Apostolic Succession is either enjoined or forbidden in the Prayer-Book, so none is enjoined or

church unity point of view, there is no need to say a word against our ritualistic friends, or to assail their view of apostolic succession. The historic episcopate is large enough to include them, and we may hope that our enlightened bishops will give them all the room they want, provided that room enough be left for those Presbyterian churchmen, otherwise called Evangelical Catholics, who gladly accept all that is transmissible from the apostles and can even admire an artistic liturgy, if not obliged to adopt all the Roman dogmas sometimes couched under its symbolism.

There is still another Presbyterian misconception as to the supposed accompaniments or consequences of the Lambeth tenets. It is feared that they are only an entering wedge, and are so bound up with the constitution of the Protestant Episcopal Church that they will yet draw after them all its legislative machinery. Well, even if that were so, an elective episcopate, with Presbyterian deputies, would not be an un-

forbidden in the Quadrilateral. It is this largeness of interpretation which makes the historic episcopate at once so ample and so tenacious a bond of church unity.

mixed calamity. It is conceivable that Presbyterians and Episcopalians might live happily together in such an American church as contrasted with the unpresbyterianized Church of England. But the truth is, that the Lambeth principles are no longer solely Anglican or American in their limitations. In considering them we are no more concerned with the Protestant Episcopal Church than with the Church of England, and no more concerned with the Church of England than with any other portion of the Catholic Church. We are only concerned with the historic episcopate as represented by the Anglican branch of it. Theoretically, we are not even concerned with the Anglican branch of it, since the same bond of church unity might be effected with the Moravian, Swedish, or Old Catholic branch of it. Practically, however, we are most naturally and hopefully concerned with our American College of Bishops, who have openly shown that they are at once the most cautious and the most progressive part of the communion to which they belong, at least as respects church unity. They have nobly taken a position outside of that communion, before the whole Christian world, as "bishops in the church of God," and are not likely now to retreat from it because of any tardy or reluctant following on the part of a school or a faction.

EPISCOPALIAN MISCONCEPTIONS

On the other side are some grave Episcopalian misconceptions which should be discussed with equal frankness. One of them is the general misapprehension of the Presbyterian idea of the Church. It seems to be assumed by our separated brethren that Presbyterians are not churchmen. Yet they claim to be good churchmen? There is not a tenet of sound churchmanship which they do not hold, and hold as tenaciously as the mass of Episcopalian churchmen. Is the test to be Catholicity, the claim to be a part of the Catholic Church? Before the Protestant Episcopal Church was born, the Presbyterian Church had defined itself in its standards as part of that "Catholic visible church into which Christ hath given the ministry, oracles, and ordinances of God." Is the test to be Apostolicity, — connection with the apostolic commission? The succession of presbyters from the apostles is undisputed throughout Christendom, even where the prelatic succession has been broken. They do not often boast of it, nor too much value it; but they have it, as a person of good descent has such a lineage, and knows that he has it, though he may not display it before the world. Lastly, is the test to be fidelity to that "sacred deposit of the primitive faith and order which Christ and his apostles committed to the Church?"[1] There is no sense in which Presbyterian ministers are not "ordained to be stewards and trustees of that deposit for the common and equal benefit of all men." Nor do they hold one another lightly to their ordination vows. They can, indeed, gladly honor the American bishops as also and pre-eminently custodians of the same deposit; and if they do not concede to them an exclusive "stewardship of grace and truth," in this opinion they are sustained by all the rest of Christendom, both Catholic and Protestant.

There is another Episcopalian misconception as to the historic liturgy contained

[1] The Preamble of the Chicago Declaration.

in the Prayer-Book. It is now held by some churchmen that the Lambeth terms are only "Catholic *minima*," which may or must draw after them a long train of other ecclesiastical requirements; and it has been surmised that the addition of the whole Prayer-Book to those terms would make their acceptance difficult, if not impossible, especially for Presbyterians. The day was, indeed, when the armed imposition of that excellent liturgy upon a Presbyterian assembly in St. Giles's Cathedral was attended with responses more forcible than decorous, and the reading of a single collect was enough to kindle a war of kingdoms as well as churches. But "the whirligig of time brings strange revenges." Let us hear the sequel: Jenny Geddes lived to throw that Presbyterian idol, her famous tripod, into a bon-fire celebrating the return of royalty, liturgy, and episcopacy.[1] It was another extreme act,

[1] "I cannot help mentioning as remarkable, that on the 23rd April, 1661, Jenny Geddes, the very woman who had given the first signal of civil broil by throwing her stool at the Dean of Edinburgh's head, when he read the service-book on the memorable 23d July, 1637, showed her conversion to loyalty by contributing the materials of her green-stall, her baskets, shells,

but the wisest and bravest act of her life, and the spirit of it worthy of some judicious imitation. It has been so imitated on the very scene of her exploit.[1] It might be so imitated in the changed circumstances of our own country. The voluntary resumption of the English Prayer-Book for optional use with more spontaneous services, would be neither inconsistent nor unseemly. There never has been any large amount of directly anti-Presbyterian material in the whole book: there is not now, two or three phrases excepted. Moreover, it was carefully revised by some of the very same Westminster divines who had framed the Presbyterian standards. As thus amended, it would be an excellent manual to accompany the Directory of Worship. No church law or good reason exists why it should not be used in every

---

forms, and even her own wicker-chair, to augment a bon-fire kindled in honor of his Majesty's coronation, and the proceedings of his Parliament." — SIR WALTER SCOTT, *Tales of a Grandfather*, Second Series, Vol. I.

[1] The Church Service Society, of which the Duke of Argyle is president, has issued an edition of the Scottish Book of Common Order, which is composed largely of portions of the English Book of Common Prayer, and is already in use in many parishes of the Established Church of Scotland.

Presbyterian Church on Fifth Avenue, or wherever else there is a state of culture requiring it. By all means let us have the Prayer-Book, "from cover to cover," [1] from its Calvinistic Declaration of absolution to its collect for instituting presbyters as ministers of the Apostolic Succession.

There is a still graver Episcopalian misconception of the motives and reasons with which the historic episcopate might be accepted. To some denominations, no doubt, it presents itself as subversive of their entire doctrine and polity, but not to the most intelligent and consistent Presbyterians. To them it would simply be a development of the apostolic presbyterate, desirable in the interest of church unity. Whenever ready to accept it, it would not be because they doubted the validity of their own ministry and sacraments: as to this they would retain the freedom of their own thoughts. It would not be solely that they might obtain certain acknowledged advantages of Episcopal church government; these they could obtain, like the

[1] A phrase used in the debates of the late Triennial Convention at Minneapolis.

Methodist Episcopalians, by developing an episcopate of their own. It would not even be that they might secure a unifying sanction to their church claims; for such a purpose other branches of the historic episcopate might yet become available. No; it would simply be, because they loyally and reverently recognize in the Anglo-American episcopate the organic centre and bond of American church unity; because they believe that episcopate has a great catholic mission, if not a scriptural warrant, to promote such unity by legitimating evangelical ministries where they are not now recognized; by giving all denominations a ministry as catholic as it is legitimate; by knitting together ecclesiastical elements, Congregational, Presbyterial, and Episcopal, which are now dismembered, and thus healing the wounds in the body of Christ; in a word, by everywhere restoring and completing the one Holy Catholic and Apostolic Church.

THE FEASIBLE EFFORT FOR UNITY.

The discussion has left but little time for the most practical part of the subject, — the methods of promoting church unity on the Lambeth basis. Unhappily, these are not yet such as to satisfy impatient minds eager for immediate results. In the present state of opinion most of us can only be Nicodemite patrons of church unity. It is too much to expect that any of us should leave popular pulpits, professional chairs, and editorial desks to embark in an anti-denominational crusade. Yet there are some things that we can do. " Without detaching ourselves from the Christian denominations to which we severally belong, or intending to compromise our relations thereto, or seeking to interfere with other efforts for Christian unity," [1] we may associate ourselves voluntarily and informally for the study of the problem with the view of educating ourselves and others toward its solution. We may not adopt the Lambeth principles outright as axioms; but we may at least " accept them as worthy of the most thoughtful consideration." [1] We may not hope for any subversion or destruction of all existing church organizations with revolutionary violence, but we may believe that " upon the basis of these principles as

[1] Declaration of the League of Catholic Unity.

articles of agreement the unification of the Christian denominations of this country may proceed, cautiously and steadily, without any alteration of their existing standards of doctrine, polity, and worship, which might not reasonably be made in a spirit of brotherly love and harmony, for the sake of unity and for the furtherance of all the great ends of the Church of Christ on earth." [1] And finally, although proposing as yet no method of carrying out these principles, we may recommend what the Lambeth Conference recommends, a comparative study of Episcopal and non-Episcopal standards of doctrine, government, and worship, with a view to their existing consensus and ultimate harmony in one Holy Catholic and Apostolic Church.

THE LEAGUE OF CATHOLIC UNITY

These are the leading features of an association known as "The League of Catholic Unity." It is the only association in existence which plants itself squarely upon the Quadrilateral basis in full accordance with the Lambeth pro-

[2] Constitution of the League of Catholic Unity.

posals. Other like associations are only in part upon that basis, or not in full accord with those proposals. Experience has shown that Church Unity societies, as composed exclusively of Episcopal clergymen, cannot, by the necessity of the case, admit non-Episcopal ministers to a frank and full discussion of the general principles of the Quadrilateral platform. Ecclesiastical conferences, like that between the Presbyterian and Episcopal commissions, though meeting on the Quadrilateral platform, are managed by representative divines, — always tenacious, sometimes justly enough tenacious, as to their respective rights and dignities. But in the Council of the Catholic League, or in one of its Local Circles, both Episcopal and non-Episcopal ministers, Congregationalists, and Presbyterians, as well as Episcopalians, may meet upon the Lambeth basis with equal rights and privileges, without restraint or embarrassment, and in a social atmosphere favorable to the utmost candor and fraternity. At the same time such a band of enthusiastic students, in such circumstances and under such influences, by their discussions and printed papers, would naturally accumulate a valuable literature as an educational agency for influencing public opinion in favor of church unity.

Without enlarging upon the mission and methods of the Catholic Unity League, I desire to recommend, not necessarily the league itself, but its principles, to the young men who are looking forward to the sacred ministry. These principles are in the spirit of that learned and catholic-minded student of the problem, the author of the "Creeds of Christendom," who has recommended Symbolic,[1] the comparative study of different church standards, as an important part of the equipment of a theological student, in view of the conflicting denominations with which he must come in contact in our country. Especially may a Presbyterian minister, while loyal to his own standards, endeavor to promote that church unity which is a cardinal principle of the Presbyterian polity, as well as the highest expression of Christian fraternity.

[1] Theological Propædeutic. By Rev. Philip Schaff, D.D., Professor in Union Theological Seminary, N. Y.

THE TRUE SPIRIT OF CHURCH UNITY

Let me add a practical word as to the duty of church unity and the spirit in which to promote it. Every day it is becoming plainer that the problem which we have been discussing is to be solved not so much by logic as by feeling, — godlike charity and brotherly love. The day for mere logic has gone by. No reasonings of ours could ever equal the reasonings of those ancestors, on the other side, who were once in so dead earnest as to exchange the pen for the sword and make martyrs of one another at the stake and upon the scaffold. Nor could any mere logic now beat down our inherited prejudices, denominational rivalries, and social jealousies. The questions which still divide us can only be settled by being ignored with mutual tolerance and left to the natural operation of the laws of thought, or rather to the supernatural influences of heaven-born charity. The Christian love which is already in our hearts must be allowed to embrace all our fellow Christians as members with us of the visible Church of Christ. The supreme test of church unity is our Saviour's own commandment, "Love thy neighbor as thyself." Do you ask in this connection, "Who is my neighbor?" Answer the question, not in the lowest sense of mere almsgiving, but in the highest sense of true charity.

Who is my neighbor? Not necessarily one who lives nigh or near me. The wayfaring Jew was in this sense no neighbor to the Samaritan. Nor can mere local neighborship exhaust church membership or church fellowship. There was indeed some plea for the local church, when it landed on the bleak New England coast, with the stormy Atlantic between it and a persecuting Christendom. But now, when that ocean is itself throbbing with electric sympathy and the whole Christian world kindling into brotherhood, the true church member whom I am to fellowship may live in Old England or in New England, next door or on the other side of the globe; if he is a fellow man and a fellow Christian, he is my neighbor.

Who is my neighbor? Not merely one who is nigh of kin, of the same blood or race. The Jew was of a different tribe or nation from the Samaritan. There were no dealings between them, or a commerce only of insults. Yet that foreigner was recognized as a neighbor. And so, mere nationality cannot limit church membership or set bounds to church catholicity. If in the old world geographical barriers and political institutions seemed to make necessary or convenient a German Church, a Dutch Church, a French Church, an English Church, a Scotch Church, yet here in this new world, with all peoples and kindreds and tongues fusing in our blood and mingling in our households, nothing human and Christian can be foreign to us. My fellow church member may be of European or American birth, of Roman, Anglican, or Scottish training; if he has the same Father in Heaven, if he is my kinsman in Christ, then he is my neighbor.

Who is my neighbor? Not exclusively one who is near to me in his belief, of the same creed or sect. The Samaritan had been excommunicated as a heretic by the Jew, whose own co-religionists, the priest and the Levite, had already passed him by in sanctimonious conceit and churchly pride. It was that difference of religion, rather than any difference of race or training, that made the victory of neighborly feeling so difficult, yet so glorious. He treated even his old persecutor as a neighbor. Ah! there may have seemed some excuse for sectarian animosity in Reformation times, when Christian men were fighting for standing room in the church of God, and Catholic and Huguenot, Cavalier and Covenanter were carving out their creeds with their swords, and illuminating them with faggots; but in this free land of free churches, with all sects and creeds shedding their errors and blending their truths in the searching light of science, learning, and thought, who of us can be infallible? The ideal churchman with whom I must be willing to fraternize may be Romanist or Protestant, Calvinist or Arminian, Congregationalist, Presbyterian, or Episcopalian, — if he is a fellow disciple of the same divine Master, if he is a fellow sinner who craves the same Saviour to atone for his errors and for mine, — then he is my neighbor.

Can you bring yourself up to the high test? Think not of some poor churchless outcast needing only your neighborly gifts of food and raiment. Think rather of some unchurching or of some unchurched brother in Christ, needing your neighborly offices of Christian love and communion. Think of some fellow Christian, who seems as far removed from your type of Christian as the Jew was from the Samaritan. Think of that " canting zealot " whom you thoroughly dislike; or of that " sentimental ritualist " whom you scornfully pity; of that " ranting revivalist; " of that " narrow Baptist; " of that " rigid Calvinist; " of that "lax Arminian ; " of that " supercilious Anglican; " of that " bigoted Romanist." Remember how the Samaritan loved the hating and hated Jew, and " Go thou and do likewise."

II

THE SIN OF SCHISM

BY THE REV. E. BENJAMIN ANDREWS, LL. D.
President of Brown University, Providence, R. I.

THE SIN OF SCHISM

"DENOMINATION" is a modern conception. The word does not occur in the New Testament, nor is the thought there to be voiced by any other word. In the sacred oracles "Church" is the great idea. Jesus Christ declared that he would found a church, and that the powers of hell should not prevail against it. The apostles seconded him in this aim, ever and everywhere toiling to add size and beauty to that divine body, the Church, whereof Christ was Head.

In New Testament conception the Church is no mere assemblage of churches, as has been sometimes imagined, as if the local church were primary and Church in the general sense secondary. The relation is precisely the reverse. The Church Catholic is always the foremost notion; so that when the church at Antioch, for instance, is spoken of, or the church at

Corinth, the idea is the Church general, so far as realized or manifested in this or that place. The Church, as viewed by the New Testament writers, is not a composite affair, made up of diverse parts, but a single, rounded totality with many facets. These facets are the local churches.

This grand, primitive view of the Church, as a seamless total, an indivisible whole, continued in the thought of thoughtful Christians until the Reformation. There were sects, of course; but most of these, if not all, had the consciousness of sects, manifesting their respect for the principle of unity by contending for the title of orthodoxy. Each thought itself right, and would put down the rest. We have before the Reformation no spectacle of various Christian bodies differing in faith and practice, yet tolerant of one another, and in some sort glad of one another's success, as is the case with the Methodist and the Presbyterian laity to-day. Denominationalism is a product of post-Reformation times. Sects were before the Reformation, denominations came after.

A "sect" is, literally, a cut, a slice. It implies out-and-out division, cleavage, resulting in the independence of the parts sundered. The word "denomination" looks more to the superficies of things, to nominal differences. It is a less radical word, giving hint of a mighty substance of belief which all denominational bodies enjoy in common. Accordant with this is the feeling of all, that sectarianism is disgraceful, but that there is no disgrace in being a stanch and loyal member of a Christian denomination.

The distinction which I make between a sect and a denomination, more fully set forth, is this, that while each admits itself to be but a part of Christendom, the denomination, renouncing all wish that one denominational organization should prevail among God's people, and viewing essential church unity as mainly a thing of faith and of spirit, not of external organization, admits not only the civil and human, but also the divine right of all the various Christian parties to exist, considering each in its time and place as a manifestation of the Divine Spirit; while the sect, on the other hand, insists that but one ecclesiastical organization ought to prevail on earth, pretends itself alone to possess the true, authoritative polity, itself alone to have the power of the keys, and berates outside Christians for not coming within the safe fold which God has set it to keep. "I am the Church," it says, "and all the rest of you, to be sure of God's favor, must change base and come over and unite with me."

In his attitude toward the Greek Church and toward Protestants, the Pope is a sectary; yet, aware of the inconsistency of assuming for his portion of Christendom the title of The One Church and yet admitting the existence of other Christians, he has always betrayed a tendency to ignore the existence of other Christians altogether. Catholics in general are with him in this; they do not like to recognize Christians who are not of their church, though, to their credit be it said, they rarely, if ever, explicitly deny that such exist.

It is the great vice of denominationalism that it tends to lapse into sectarianism, to ignore the Church's unity, so leading to the sin of schism. This is the characteristic guilt of the ultra-Protestant world to-day, of Lutherans, Baptists, Congregationalists, Presbyterians, and Methodists. We have a sharp sense of denomination, but almost no sense of church.

The ordinary denominationalist now has no feeling for the old Catholic Church. Usually he hates and despises it. He remembers that it bred Leo X., but forgets that it raised up Luther, Calvin, and Knox. I know of no sadder mistaking of history than that involved in current Protestant notions of what the Church was and was doing in the years before Luther. Doubtless very grave evils prevailed then, more in church administration than in the lives of Christian people, and far more in connection with the Papal See than in church administration at large. Yet, with all its errors, that old Church was God's Church, and the net influence of it was not evil, but gloriously good. Its doctrines were in the main biblical and reasonable. It taught the unity of God, the person and work of Christ, the power of the atonement, man's guilt and man's hope. These truths were not only held creedwise; they were preached, by earnest men and with saving effect. The Reformation brought to the parts of Christendom which it affected immense advance in all these respects; still it is very easy, as it is very usual, to underrate the evangelical excellence of the church in which Luther had his spiritual birth.

Nor did the reformers export from that old Church all the good it contained. Men as holy as they preferred to remain in it; men as holy as they have been in the old establishment ever since. I am strong Protestant enough not to be afraid to admit that there are at this moment multitudes of true and faithful Christians in the Romish communion. It is part of that Holy Catholic Church in which we all believe. I would speak and think respectfully even of the Pope. He is head pastor of one of the oldest, noblest, and most useful congregations on earth, the one to which St. Paul directed the epistle reproduced in our Bibles. We may duly abominate the papal system and the papal claims without calling the Pope Antichrist or unchurching the hosts of Christians who see in his hands the keys of St. Peter.

Many Protestants commit the sin of schism in the attitude they assume toward one another. The great bodies of Protestant people are mutually friendly enough. Most of us, when we as individuals pray for the Holy Catholic Church, have before our minds a most inclusive thought. We take into our affections Catholic and Greek, Lutheran, Anglican, and Presbyterian, Baptist, Methodist, Quaker, Plymouth Brother, and Soldier of the Salvation Army; and probably no one of us, in such a prayer, ever entertains the idea that these fellow Christians, to be blessed as we pray, must adopt this or that ecclesiastical costume.

But no way has yet been found to realize this splendid width of charity in church practice. Our ecclesiastical machinery forbids. It is too stiff. Church officials almost always manifest a sectarian consciousness. In its administration, direction, and public spirit, nearly every Protestant body is a sect rather than a denomination. Many of the laity themselves, however catholic in their personal feelings and thinking, still regard so sacred each his special mode of church building, that they will plan to defend and bolster it even when souls are visibly perishing in consequence of such narrowness. The Pope is not a whit stiffer in this than thoughtless Protestants are.

Forgetting that under any one's theory church polity is naught but a means, good people in effect make it an end. That is the sectary's fallacy.

Very strong denominational feeling always tends to become sectarian. While, as has been said, the laymen of the Christian world are usually not so, church officials are very commonly sectarian in thought and speech. Nearly all our Protestant religious newspapers speak as the organs of sects rather than of denominations. Each claims for its party in some sense the power of the keys. I am acquainted with ministers whose glee would be keener at welcoming into their churches Christians of other names than if they were permitted to baptise so many heathen. Communities are not rare in this land where competition is far sharper between the different denominations than between Christ's kingdom and Satan's.

Of course, so long and so far as this spirit prevails, denominations have no chance to come by any better understanding of one another's grounds for their peculiar contentions than they now have; no opportunity, should any of these grounds lose force owing to lapse of time or change of circumstances, to see this, so that divisions might cease when no longer called for.

It seems to be the common view that a denomination, in order to promote to the utmost its peculiar tenets, must separate itself as completely as possible from all who reject these tenets. That is, if certain Christian people entertain what you call errors, you cannot duly testify against those errors without excluding those people from your church. To my mind this is wholly wrong. The logic of it is that to influence men with my truth I must put them as far as possible away from me. Nothing could be more senseless. Of what use, in a congregation where all believe in it, is a sermon, for instance, on immersion? Were we nearer together, more mixed up, as it were, such a shot would find its mark. The crisp cleavage between denominations involves a double disadvantage. Important specialties in faith remain too much without influence, and pernicious oddities too much without rebuke. Of course "birds of a feather will flock together." Those who agree in belief will ever tend to affiliate.

Let them do so by all means. But they need not be bulkheaded off from others. We have sets and stripes in our American society, but as yet, thank God, no castes. So should it be in religious organization.

Sectarianism is to blame for it that we do not have better union, direction, and system in city evangelization, in religious effort for country communities, and in planting Christianity on our Western frontier. To our shame be it said, the utmost cross purposes and confusion prevail in these fields. Throughout the work of Protestant churches there is almost total lack of co-ordination, hardly a trace of that order and economy which enable the Romanists to accomplish such wonders with their slender resources. In cities, numerous powerful congregations huddle together where one of them could do as much good as all do now. Every mission field in a wealthy neighborhood is fought for by a half score of denominations, while the dives and slums are neglected about in proportion to their need. In each country town two, four, six, sometimes eight or ten apologies for churches try to live where one strong one would suffice; where, moreover, such strong church could easily be built up by combination of effort, and where, being erected, it would have ten times the saving power which all the weaklings at present exert.

In almost any of the rising towns of the West you may see a sight which Christendom entire ought not to show, — from half a dozen to a dozen struggling churches, with under-fed ministers, inadequate accommodations, and a discouraging outlook every way, much of such meagre support as they do receive coming from the East, not one among them powerful or promising enough to entice the lukewarm or to make evil-doers reflect. Christians moving to the place, seeing the financial burden it must entail to join any of the churches, remain churchless; while the unbeliever, who would under other circumstances at least send his children to Sunday School and occasionally go to church himself, lapses into heathenism with all his house.

Many, if not most, of our poorer rural and frontier communities are threatened with desperate apathy touching religion; a practical infidelity, carrying with it the grossest immoralities. In many parts these evils are already realized. No centralized embodiment of spiritual force, like "The Church" of the middle ages, is available for combating them. It is doubtful whether the expression, "The Church," has, to the ordinary man of the world, any meaning whatever. If he frames a thought corresponding with it, he probably thinks of the Roman Catholic Church, which, if he is not a Catholic, awakens in him no veneration, lays upon his conscience no restraint, no commandment.

Yet, in the face of the perils referred to, religious teachers, each in his little patch of the Lord's vineyard, serenely go on, inculcating the old divisive church polity, unfortunately having influence enough to continue the anarchy, and even to invest it, in the minds of many excellent Christians, with a sort of sacredness. Nine tenths of the good people thus preventing each other from religious usefulness no doubt surmise their error, and might easily be led to act differently; but, not being experts in theology, they suppose their present course somehow right because the ecclesiastical authorities over them approve it, particularly as, by sedulous begging in remote places, where the state of affairs is not known, those authorities manage to provide them with goodly sums of money to sink. It is by this flagitious anarchy that Protestants continually play into the hands of the Catholic Church. We shall have increasing cause to dread papal supremacy in America so long as our religious resources are thus foolishly and criminally frittered away. Were denominations less far apart, this evil would not be. Nothing is responsible for it but our painful preference of Shibboleth to salvation. Our foreign missionaries have set us a noble example in this matter. They parcel out the field, and no man builds on another's foundation. We shall one day learn the same wisdom at home.

This persistent idea of the power of the keys at first seems hard to understand. It goes back, however, to the notion of a divine ecclesiastical legitimacy. Most Protestants are of the opinion, or at least have been until recently, that Christ, in the New Testament, ordains a given fixed ecclesiastical polity for all time. The Papists, and, in part, the Episcopalians, locate the divine authority for their polity in the Church, somewhat independently of Scripture. Of course, if there is committed to us any definite polity prescribed in perpetuity, with the seal of divine authority upon it, then we must maintain that polity at whatever cost. We must cling to it ourselves; we must fight for it against those trying to subvert it. Any church, any sect supposing itself in possession of a divinely ordained form of church building, cannot do otherwise than maintain such, though it should seem to work, though it should confessedly and certainly work divisively in Christendom. Upon that theory we should have to say, "God's will be done," though the results at present, to all human appearance, are the reverse of helpful to the progress of his kingdom. He knows best, and who are we that our finite judgments should presume to dictate to infinite wisdom? If your polity can be shown to be divinely legitimate, you, of course, have the power of the keys; and you have no option but to assert and maintain that power against all comers. Here is the heart of our difficulty.

For my part I deny, root and branch, the

doctrine of a primordial ecclesiastical legitimacy. No special form of polity is prescribed in the New Testament. In the New Testament as a whole, no special form is exemplified. Germs of all forms are there, but no one is carried through to the exclusion of the others. In the group of bishop-elders with which every New Testament church, however small, is fitted out, you have the presbytery. The church of Jerusalem, of Antioch, of Corinth, or of Rome at the time of Paul's death, — the one church in each of these cities comprising numerous congregations, and the board of bishop-elders in each probably having by this time a more or less permanent chairman, — gives you a picture of an Episcopalian diocese. Throughout the Asiatic circle all the churches recognize a centre of paramount authority in the church at Jerusalem, which church, on occasion, assumes to issue *dogmata*, or authoritative prescriptions, which all are to keep. In this department of primitive Christendom, moreover, James, who is neither bishop nor elder, whose name is also an official title, almost like Cæsar's, has something the authority of a pope. In the Pauline or European circle, on the other hand, in the first age of Christianity, all the churches are independent of one another, like Baptist and Congregational churches to-day; and the *dogmata* issued at Jerusalem, though exactly fitting difficulties that arose in the church at Corinth, are unknown or ignored by the apostle when treating of those difficulties.

There is no ground whatever in Scriptural precept or example for asserting any form of polity as particularly legitimate. The Romanist is correct in alleging that authority has been lodged in the Church to work out its own polity; but he has no right to say that his one department of the Church is a law, or can give law, to all Christendom. His church constitution is good for him, no doubt; it is good, and any form of polity is good, so far as it works well. The note of church legitimacy is doing church work. Any organization bearing this mark, however imperfect its means, however humble its aspect, is a legitimate part of the one Church, and must not be despised.

The great demand of religion in the Protestant world to-day is that the Christian denominations should entirely cease claiming the power of the keys; leave off being sects, and come up to their ideal as only so many facets of the Holy Catholic Church. I do not say that this renewed sense of church is all that is needed in the direction of church unity. I allege only that this is our prime and generic necessity. Denominational federation, or the extension of the historic episcopate, may follow; nay, something in the way of fuller organization will be sure to follow. But it is useless to attempt reform in external organization among the churches till a healthy ecclesiastical consciousness is born again. Christendom needs once more the old sense of love for all God's people by all God's people. We are not enemies, but friends. What unites us is far more important than what divides.

Nor is there necessarily any incompatibility between the fact of denominations and the sense of catholicity. I would not have denominations cease to be; an attempt to abolish them were equally foolish and vain. But I would have each see itself in its right relations to the rest, lay aside all arrogance and sense of superior-ity; in a word, all claim to the power of the keys, recognizing the rest, more than we do, as allies, that we might toil in a more united way than now for the establishment of God's kingdom among men.

To see how possible it would be to preserve denominations in all their useful meaning, yet all of them renouncing the power of the keys, we have only to generalize in thought what goes on in every religious organization, however diminutive, to-day. Each of them has its high church, low church, and broad church party, its progressive and its conservative tendency. In one congregation nearly all are advanced thinkers; in another almost all fear and deprecate innovation. One runs to ritual; another subordinates or abhors ritual. In a community of size, containing several congregations of the same faith and order, these likes and dislikes get themselves humored by a natural process of grouping. Harmony is easy then. But even in smaller places, where people of divergent tastes form one congregation, though they may debate and strive, each stripe trying to impart its color to the whole, such rivalry hardly ever passes the limit of health or leads to division. Even when the tension is extreme and one section or another secedes, the seceders hardly ever presume to originate a new sect. The separation leads neither side to unchurch the other. If they were Lutherans before, both are Lutherans still; if Disciples, Disciples; if Baptists, Baptists; and so on. What reason is there, I ask, but the pride and folly of good men, why this fraternal shading and grouping of Christian bodies should not extend throughout Christendom? We easily generalize it in thought; why may it not be made general in fact?

To see in another way that this is a distinct possibility one need only recur to the time in the old Catholic Church before the papacy acquired its supremacy, say in the days of Cyprian. Then the sense of church, of catholicity, was as high as it has ever been, while every bishopric claimed the right to act and grow in its own way, subject only to the authority of general councils. Let us suppose that this order of things had continued and developed, and that councils had always declined to assume authority save in absolutely fundamental matters of faith. All peculiarities of belief, of practice, and of polity would then have been free to work themselves out. After a time, hardly two congregations would have agreed in all things. National and local churches would have had their dissidencies of view, just as they have had. There would have been parties and tendencies of all sorts. Calvinism when it came would have had its champions and its opponents, each side free to say its last word. When diversities of belief and practice grew too tense in any local church some would freely withdraw to cast in their lot elsewhere. Here would be a congregation of ritualists, yonder one worshipping like Quakers or the Plymouth Brethren. Every biblical truth, every extreme, every folly, every error, even, would be represented somewhere. Yet nowhere would there be exclusion. Extremes of view and of organization would shade off gradually, and you would seek in vain for any of that crisp cleavage of party from party which characterizes sects. No section or tendency would claim to be the Church. No man would unchurch another. No church dignitary would pretend, in the papal sense, to bind or to loose.

Some model like this, it seems to me, ought denominationalism to hold before itself, as the goal for its advance. To a goodly extent we realize it already, and if the great commonalty of Protestant Christians were free to act out its best spirit we should realize it perfectly. But there still remains in the government of all denominations a certain thought of authority, an unvoiced but potent claim to the power of the keys, an unclear yet positive assumption of special ecclesiastical legitimacy, which makes impossible that useful harmony and co-operation which but for this we could so easily effect. More than for all else do I blame Rome for ending that beautiful old ecclesiastical development to which I have alluded, introducing the exercise of ecclesiastical power, and so familiarizing the Church with it that no denomination yet, however ultra its Protestantism, has felt free to renounce the assumption of it.

I believe, no less than a papist, in the organic unity of God's people; for faith organically connects all who possess it into one vital body. But this organic unity need not carry with it any particular machinery of ecclesiastical organization. External organization is a different, a much coarser thing. For my part, I repudiate utterly the notion that the unity which our Lord prayed for on behalf of his Church is primarily unity in external, visible organization. Such unity is not the main matter, not the most necessary, not the most desirable attainment. What we need first and most is unity of spirit in the bond of peace.

Church organization is important, in some ages all-important. Every church polity that ever existed, the papal system included, has had, or still has, its relative justification. It is with polities as with doctrinal statements. All of them that have ever found currency anywhere in the Church had in their time and place some measure of truth, some sort of propriety. They were the natural and inevitable results springing from the operation of Christian truth upon men's minds so and so educated, developed, and influenced.

But Christian humanity, like all humanity, "sweeps onward," and governments and creeds which once were the best possible expression of divine faith become outworn and uncouth. In the advance, one division of the faithful will be the first to spy out a new truth, another will do equal good by tenaciously holding on to some rubric which the rest were too ready to dismiss. Each will of coarse be strenuous for the aspects of truth which most separate it from the rest, but not one will have any right to call itself pre-eminently the Church of God, whether in polity or in doctrine. If any does so, if any excludes its neighbor, saying: You neglect this or that important item of belief, therefore you are not of the Church; if any in any way claims the power of the keys, we shall look upon such assumption precisely as we do upon that of the Pope, as insufferable arrogance, proof that the perfect vision of Christ's mind has not yet come to all.

The renunciation of sectarianism is, then, the first and great duty of the Church in view of its dividedness. A correct idea and feeling must be built up touching the meaning of "church." If this cannot be effected, all effort will be vain. So long as any party of Christians says, — "We practise so and so, and are therefore preeminently *the* Church; we are the Church and you are not," — scorning or patronizing others who produce all the fruits of the spirit; — so long must the reunion of Christendom wait. Even were it known that the episcopate would prove the church unifying force which so many hope, churchmen would not on that account be justified in calling themselves the Church *par excellence*. Speaking generally, no denominations are at this moment to be reprehended for existing apart. If a few are to-day in fault for this, very few, certainly, were to blame for coming into existence in the first place. Nearly every rent in the Church has occurred for good conscience' sake, a new party forming because the old body was too arrogant. Any thought about the reunion of Christendom which expects it to occur by come-outers' retracing their steps is wholly fatuous. We shall never arrive at unity by arbitrarily suppressing the peculiarities of this or that denomination. If Catholicity is ever to return to the Church, it will have to be vastly larger and more comprehensive than ever existed before. It must be immense enough to include us all, pretty much as we are. It will have to consist mainly in a new spirit, as I have said; in the better way in which we shall regard, approach, and help one another.

As it is not possible, so neither is it necessary or desirable that the various denominations should merge into a homogeneous body. All need not teach the same views concerning either doctrine or polity. What is needed is that all church people as such should come to believe — effectively — what nearly all even now privately acknowledge, that polity is good for nothing save as an instrument in the Church's saving work; that church orders and ordinances were made for men, not men for them. Let this truth be taken up into Christian teaching everywhere, and the Christian love in good men's hearts will spontaneously prompt them, whenever the two interests clash, to subordinate mere matters of polity to the promotion of truth, the salvation of wicked men, and the edification of good men.

A main reason why proper catholicity in feeling is so desirable is that it would bring certain needed changes in churches' external relations. We see this in the pleasing fact that no sooner does the need of church unity begin to be earnestly discussed than you have the Young Men's Christian Association, the Evangelical Alliance, with the local denominational alliances to which it is now happily giving birth, the Grindelwald Conference, originated and inspired by Dr. Lunn, the great Society of Christian Endeavorers, and a thousand other forms of interdenominational co-operation, reciprocity, and comity which recently did not exist. This movement will be extended further.

A plan so simple that it has occurred even to me would, if carried out, as it has begun to be, annul many baneful results of present schism.

Let the denominations represented in any State each elect one well-known minister and one well-known layman to serve with similar officers from the other denominations, upon a State Advisory Church Advancement Committee. Let this committee diligently look over the newest fields and publish opinions like the following: In our judgment the religious welfare of Beatifica, in the county of Gaudium, requires that for the present all Christian residents in the place assist the Methodists, the Methodists there having gotten the strongest foothold. In our judgment, the religious welfare of Gloriana, the rapidly growing shire town of Excelsior County, demands that all shall aid the Presbyterians of the place. And so on. In due time churches of other faiths could be approbated in these same localities. All would be informal, unauthoritative, non-compulsory, the system acting by moral force and public sentiment alone.

What would be the result of such a policy? Instead of many spindling plants, each town would soon have at least one strong church, with an able ministry, a flourishing Sunday School, good music, and desirable accommodations of every kind. Cold Christians and the worldly would be attracted, unbelief would be matched, and the kingdom of God would grow apace. I am not without hope of living to see this scheme in happy exercise over considerable territory. If I die without the sight, some of you will not.

Denominations will still stand, and each have an even better chance than now to show what grace is in it; but, in case the response becomes general, feeble, dying churches will be far less numerous in our hamlets and border settlements; city congregations will cease to crowd each other; co-operation will supplant anarchy; all missionary fields will be cultivated up to the limit of the resources of the total church; immense economies in the way of theological teaching, and missionary, educational, and philanthropic machinery will be introduced; and the golden age of perfected humanity be hastened in a thousand ways.

After all this is done, however, much will probably remain undone. Certain real modifications of church organization will no doubt ultimately be required to give the coming catholicity practical effect. Mere correct feeling, theory, and doctrine, with comity and casual co-operation, will not suffice. The spirit of comprehension must and will create itself organs whereby to act upon the world.

However, touching the changes needed by the Church in its essential constitution, many intelligent writers seem to me to express themselves rashly. All have read utterances to the effect that one sole external church organization ought to have absolutely ecumenical application. I cannot view it so. The United States need not be bound together with Europe in church organization. The spirit of true catholicity must of course reach to the ends of the earth; but nothing is to be gained, and perhaps much would be lost, by placing the whole Christian earth under one ecclesiastical government, however simple and unauthoritative. Nor is it necessary that your outer *régime* should be stringently universal even within a given land or State. If the visible union involves the great majority of Christians; if it is only comprehensive enough to give the word " Church " a clear and emphatic meaning in the minds of all; powerful enough to form a hold for Christian thought and to organize Christian work, — then a thin fringe of schismatic growth about the great ecclesiastical field can occasion no harm. I feel that distinct provision should be made for a liberty like this; for there will always be some whom the general church administration will not please; who, therefore, may wish to stand outside it for a time or permanently. No constraint must be applied to such to make them conform. Were the reunion of Christendom to cost any impairment of religious liberty, most of us would prefer that it should not come.

Another observation helps show that the task of absolutely necessary unification in church externals is less impossible than it at first seems. While nearly every denomination in Christendom was justified in beginning to be, time has in many directions so far removed denominational differences that nothing but tradition now prevents fusion. The Baptists and the Free Baptists well illustrate this. There is no longer any propriety whatever in their apartness. The regular Baptists are no longer exclusively Calvinistic, nor do they uniformly practise or insist upon close communion. These two bodies could blend without the slightest surrender or sacrifice on the part of either, and with the greatest blessing to both. Little if any higher is the fence between Baptists and Congregationalists. Both have the same doctrines and the same polity. Nothing separates them except differences as to the form, and, in part, as to the subjects of baptism. But these differences did not at first or for a long time divide them, and have never, to this day, caused the entire separation of the two bodies in Great Britain. Likely enough, were these denominations to unite, many a congregation would be made up mainly of immersionists, many another mainly of non-immersionists, just as now within the Baptist denomination particular congregations vary greatly from one another in their thought and practice about communion. Some friction would naturally arise from these diverse procedures, but the danger from this source is certainly not sufficient to justify in this age the out-and-out duality of two Christian bodies so closely akin to one another.

This union being effected, there would be beautiful hope of coalescence between the body thus formed and the Presbyterians. The notion of presbytery is not strange to Congregationalists or to Baptists. Those who wish episcopacy generalized lay stress upon its early origin and very wide prevalence in the Church. But the presbyter is at once a more ancient and a more ubiquitous functionary than the bishop in the Episcopalian sense of that word. The only important separatrix between Congregationalists and Baptists on the one hand and Presbyterians on the other, regards the authority of the general body over the particular congregation. But even here the difference is much less wide than it seems, since both Baptists and Congregationalists have for many years been developing a central power which in fact, though not in theory, to a great extent commands the particular churches.

There would thus be formed an immense presbytero-Congregational ecclesiasticism standing face to face with a mighty Episcopal ecclesiasticism made up of all the churches that are governed by bishops; for these too, must, in time, draw together into practical working unity. Well, will these ecclesiasticisms stand apart forever, or will further blending occur, making one that colossal twain? I am of opinion that that last chasm will at length be closed, and American Christendom be made one indeed. Ecclesiastical overseership is really very important. Here the bishop's polity has, for practical work, an immense advantage. All will one day see this. The bishops' churches, knowing it already, will be so anxious for the generalization of the overseership that they will not be too scrupulous about the manner of effecting the consummation.

By and by, I believe, the Chicago-Lambeth overture will bear fruit. All are acquainted with the nature of this. The Anglican Council, consisting of all the Protestant Episcopal bishops of Great Britain, the British colonies, and the United States, in 1888, at the last of the three meetings, — it was held at Lambeth Palace, London, the meeting being attended by one hundred and forty-five bishops of Great Britain and America, — adopted, with slight modifications, a programme for the reunion of Christendom, which had, in 1886, been proposed by the House of Bishops in the General Convention of the Protestant Episcopal Church of the United States. This programme consists of four articles : —

"I. The Holy Scriptures of the Old and New Testaments, as 'containing all things necessary to salvation,' and as being the rule and ultimate standard of faith.

"II. The Apostles' Creed, as the Baptismal Symbol; and the Nicene Creed, as the sufficient statement of the Christian faith.

"III. The two Sacraments ordained by Christ himself, — Baptism and the Supper of the Lord, — ministered with the unfailing use of Christ's words of institution, and of the elements ordained by him.

"IV. The Historic Episcopate, locally adapted in the methods of its administration to the varying needs of the nations and peoples called of God into the unity of his Church.

"This conference," — so runs the overture, — "earnestly requests the constituted authorities of the various branches of our communion, acting, as far as may be, in concert with one another, to make it known that they hold themselves in readiness to enter into brotherly conference (such as that which has already been proposed by the Church in the United States of America) with the representatives of other Christian communions in the English-speaking races in order to consider what steps can be taken, either toward corporate reunion, or toward such relations as may prepare the way for fuller organic unity hereafter."

The first and third of these articles are already agreed upon by all Protestants;

while the creeds named in Article II. might easily be so modified as not to exclude even Unitarian Christians. Serious friction arises only touching the episcopate; and at present this is serious indeed. Most non-Episcopalians deem the bishops intent merely on getting Nonconformists under their authority, while many Episcopalians think the Lambeth proposals a mistake anyway, and charge the bishops who published them with recreancy to church principles. At any rate, it is said, the bishops must admit to their orders only such non-Episcopal ministers as renounce their non-Episcopal ordination. Few of the Presbyterian, Congregational, or Baptist clergy will ever do this. But a great many clergymen in these bodies stand ready, for the sake of promoting church unity, to take bishops' orders so soon as any bishops are ready to ordain them, with the understanding that their original ordination is not abjured; and so soon, further, as such enlarged ordination is reasonably likely not to result in merely creating a new denomination. The conditions for this momentous step toward the final church polity do not yet exist. The men who framed the League of Catholic Unity know this full well. Sectarianism is still too rife. Years, decades perhaps, must roll away before so splendid a consummation can be reached. But this immense good is surely in store for the Church because it is Christ's Church, and because Christ, through his Church, is pledged to convert the world to himself.

III

THE IRENIC MOVEMENTS SINCE THE REFORMATION

By the Rev. JOHN F. HURST, D.D., LL. D.

Bishop of the Methodist Episcopal Church, Washington, D. C.

THE IRENIC MOVEMENTS SINCE THE REFORMATION

WHEN the great Reformation came to a close, the spirit of controversy prevailed everywhere on the map of the new Protestantism. The Reformed were in the ascendency in Switzerland, in Southern Germany, in Holland and Scotland. The Lutherans predominated in Central Germany and in the Scandinavian countries. The press teemed with controversial discussions. The atmosphere of the universities was lurid with the violent storm. Only at intervals was a strong word spoken for the harmony of Protestantism. Melanchthon had been the one peaceful spirit of the Reformation, but this irenic character of the man did not avail to calm the troubled waters of the period. The question was, How long must the Protestantism of the continent wait for an advocate of union, and who should be the man?

The earliest apostle of Christian union was George Calixtus. At the University of Helmstädt, where he was professor, 1614–1656, he became imbued with the Melanchthonian theology, and by his wide travels in England, Holland, Italy, and France, he formed a larger acquaintance with other churches than was common with either the Lutherans or Reformed of his day. This brought him to a breadth of view far in advance of his time. He was an earnest Lutheran, always maintaining that the Lutheran Church was the purest of all. But he saw the transcendent importance of those great doctrines on which all Protestants were agreed, and he laid down as a basis of Christian union the New Testament as interpreted by the Church of the first five centuries. He contended that the points on which the churches differed were unimportant by the side of the fundamental points of Christian theology which they had inherited in common from the purest ages of the faith. The churches should work together in peace and harmony, paving the way for a possible union. Calixtus did not at first advocate a formal union. A conference for Christian union was appointed at Thorn in 1645, but nothing came of it except as a wise and pacific example. The strict Lutherans opposed him with intense bitterness. He was called by some a Crypto-Calvinist, by others a secret Papist. It is pathetic to read how the well-meant efforts of the Helmstädt peacemaker were frustrated and denounced by the vehement controversialists of that age. Walch called him Calixtus Cal(vino m)ixtus, and identified him with the number of the beast in the Apocalypse. It was a militant age, and the peacemaker's rôle was not popular.[1]

The theological school of Frankfort-on-the-Oder was a centre of a peace movement. There it was that Bergius and Francus labored for a tolerant Calvinism, and spoke many a noble word for peace in the former half of the seventeenth century. There also Pelargus seconded their efforts, and was a powerful irenic influence. It

[1] Henke, Georg Calixtus und seine Zeit, Halle, 1853, and art. in Herzog-Plitt; Dowding, Life and Correspondence of G. Calixtus, Lond., 1863; Gieseler, iv. 584 ff. (Smith); art. in McClintock and Strong, ii. 30; Hallam, Lit. of Europe, ii. 401–404, and notes.

is interesting to think of this school at Frankfort-on-the-Oder standing in the same relation to the Reformed Church and to the Lutheran as Union Theological Seminary stands to the Old and New School Presbyterians, — dedicated to peace and compromise from its very origin. It was this same Frankfort group which first gave publicity to that golden word: "In necessary things unity, in things indifferent liberty, in all charity." This is the noble motto of the Evangelical Alliance. We are indebted to Richard Baxter for introducing this sentence to the English world, which he does in his "True and Only Way of Concord of All Christian Churches."[1] There Baxter says: "Were there no more said of all this subject but that of Rupertus Meldenius, cited by Conradus Bergius, it might end all schism if well understood and used, viz.: *Si in necessariis sit unitas, in non-necessariis libertas, in utrisque caritas, optimo certe loco essent res nostrae*,— Unity in things necessary, Liberty in things unnecessary, and Charity in both, would do all our work." A professor in Union Seminary has the honor of first

[1] London, 1680.

tracing this word to its origin. In the summer of 1887 Dr. Briggs searched through the libraries of Germany until he found a copy of the anonymous book, "Paraenesis Votiva," which is the source of this immortal sentence, and which book is referred by Bergius to Rupertus Meldenius. The probable date is 1627. As Professor Briggs remarks, the author does not belong to men of fame. He passed away in obscurity. But his words remain, to fructify in a better soil, and to bring forth fruit in a better age. And this word of his should keep his name in everlasting remembrance.[1]

John Durie was the greatest peacemaker of the seventeenth century. The same scholar already mentioned has the honor of calling the attention of the American Church to this indefatigable laborer for church union.[2] Durie, who was probably

---

[1] See Briggs, in Presb. Rev. 1887, pp. 496 ff., 743 ff.

[2] Briggs, The Work of John Durie in behalf of Christian Union in the Seventeenth Century: Presb. Rev. viii. 297-309. Here is published for the first time Durie's Summaric Relation of his Work for Ecclesiastical Pacification from July, 1631, until September, 1633, from an original manuscript of Durie, discovered by Dr. Briggs, and now in the library of Union Seminary.

a Scotchman, first meets us at Elbing, Prussia, where he was pastor of an English factory. There he became acquainted with Godeman, a privy counsellor of Gustavus Adolphus. Godeman suggested to Durie that whoever should bring about a reconciliation between the great parties into which Christendom was divided would be the greatest peacemaker. This remark was the turning point of his life. In 1628 he addressed a letter to the Swedish king, "for the obtaining of aid and assistance in this seasonable time, to seek for and re-establish an ecclesiastical peace among the evangelical churches." The king gave his sanction, and gave him letters recommending him to all Protestant princes. Henceforth he devoted his life to this work. He went to and fro between England and the continent, attending assemblies, receiving opinions, exhorting to union, trying to bring about reconciliation of differences, and looking for a common platform on which all could stand. Some English bishops, — even Laud, then Bishop of London, — looked with great favor on his work. Bishops Davenant, Morton, and Hall gave him their views on Christian union, which were published in 1634. Bishop Davenant's statement is one of the most valuable contributions to Christian union ever published. It contains this noble sentence: "True and genuine charity is no less necessary to salvation for all churches and members of Christian churches than the true and entire profession of sound and saving faith." Many of the most eminent divines in England gave a hearty God-speed to Durie. It is interesting to notice so early as this a sincere longing for Christian union on the part of many of the leading spirits both in the English Church and on the continent. A meeting of the Protestant states at Frankfort, in 1634, passed a resolution indorsing Durie: "They did judge his work most laudable, most acceptable to God, and most necessary and useful to the Church." In 1640 he presented a petition to the House of Commons, urging "that the blessed and long-sought-for union of Protestant churches might be recommended unto the publick prayers of the Church, and that his majesty with your honours advice and counsell might be moved to call a general Synod of Protestants in due time for the better settling of weighty matters in the Church, which now trouble not only the conscience of most men, but disturb the tranquility of publick states, and divide the churches from one another, to the great hindrance of Christianity and the dishonour of religion." And so he labored on through his long and restless life, having only one object, — the pacification of the churches, and their restoration to ancient unity. He was charged by William Prynne with being "the time-serving Proteus and ambidexter divine;" but defended himself as "the unchanged, constant, and single-hearted peacemaker." His principles were: —

"(1) A full body of practical divinity, which instead of the ordinary philosophical jangling school divinity, might be proposed to all those that seeke the truth, which is after godlinesse.

"(2) To abolish the names of parties, as presbyterial, prelatical, congregational, etc., and to be called Reformed Christians of England, Scotland, France, Germany, etc.

"(3) To discountenance controversial writings by private persons.

"(4) It is the mind of Christ that his servants in all matters merely circumstantiall by him not determined should be left free to follow their own light, as it may be offered, or arise unto them, from the general rules of edification and not constrained by an implicit faith to follow the dictates of other men."

This great apostle of Christian union died in 1680, without seeing the fruits of his labors. The times were too turbulent and the age was not ripe for his pacific ideas. Gieseler says he received much more encouragement from the Reformed than from Lutherans. He was three hundred years in advance of his age. But, as Professor Briggs says, "He was sowing the seed and preparing the germs of Christian toleration, liberty, and union that have unfolded in later time and richer promises for the future."[1] Many of the best spirits of his time gave him encouragement, and his numerous books and his tireless labors form one of the noblest legacies which

[1] For further information, see Briggs, as above; Gieseler (ed. Smith), iv. 583-584; Briggs, in Schaff-Herzog, s. v.; McClintock, in McClintock and Strong, s. v., and the references there given. See also The Christian Remembrancer, January, 1855, where a full account is given, written from the sources.

church history has bequeathed us from the seventeenth century.

Hugo Grotius, a contemporary of Calixtus, was also enamoured of the idea of a united Christendom. He differed from Calixtus in this: that while Calixtus was a stanch Protestant, and made his concessions not toward Rome, but toward Geneva, and contented himself with trying to bring the Reformed and the Lutherans to a common understanding, Grotius turned rather toward Rome, and advocated a restored and purified Catholicism, as a common solvent of all sects, and a large fold for the peaceable meeting-place of all Christians. This strange reversion on Grotius's part to the Roman Church as the hope of Christendom, may be explained from two facts: (1) Grotius was an Arminian. He was delighted to find, as he thought, that the stern doctrines of Calvin were absent from the ancient fathers, that Jerome and Chrysostom and the Catholic fathers knew nothing of these tenets. This led him to a passionate rebound in favor of antiquity. (2) The iron of the Protestant intolerance had entered into his own soul. After his escape from prison he had taken refuge in France, where he was received with open arms. The cordial attitude of the Catholic ecclesiastics softened the rigidity of his Protestantism. As Hallam says: "The ill usage he sustained at the hands of those who boasted their independence of Papal tyranny; the caresses of the Gallican clergy after he had fixed his residence at Paris; the growing dissensions and virulence of the Protestants; the choice that seemed alone to be left in their communion between a fanatical anarchy, disintegrating everything like a church on the one hand, and a domination of bigoted and vulgar ecclesiastics on the other, made him gradually less and less averse to the comprehensive and majestic unity of the Catholic hierarchy, and more and more willing to concede some point of uncertain doctrine, or some form of ambiguous expression."[1] By ample quotations from his epistles Hallam has proved this defection of Grotius. But it was in the interest of a large union. He thought the Swedish, the English, and the Danish churches might come together, under a revived and reformed Catholic banner. He

[1] Lit. of Europe, ii. 397–398.

was weary of dissension. He wanted peace. But he wrote rather as a statesman than a theologian. It was peace at the expense of truth; it was peace at the expense of the fullest liberty of private judgment. Grotius did not himself go so far as to make the last sacrifice of his own conscience by accepting the infallibility of the Roman Church. Whether he would have done so had he lived, it is useless to inquire. His scheme was a vision, an hallucination. The history of Roman Catholicism for the last three hundred years has proven that.

John Owen, the greatest of the Puritan divines, the Nestor of the Congregationalists, in his treatise on schism, lays down a liberal platform. He holds that the true and essential note of the Church of Christ is union with Christ, "and wherever there is a man, or a body of men, who are united to Him by living faith, and are keeping his commandments, he or they are in communion with the Church of God." "He belongs to the Church catholic," runs his noble charter, "who is united to Christ by the spirit, and none other."[1] He vin-

[1] Works, Ed. Russell, xix. 253.

dicated boldly the right of the Nonconformist churches to exist, and yet in an irenical spirit, and as one sincerely desiring the union of all Christians in England. Thus in his vindication of the Nonconformists from the charge of schism, an answer to a sermon by Stillingfleet (1680), he deprecates religious controversy in the interest of Protestant union, and says that in the presence of the common danger of the Roman Church the sharp words of Stillingfleet are unseasonable.[1] But he had no faith in artificial schemes of union. He says: "I should be very sorry that any man living should outgo me in desires that all who fear God throughout the world, especially in these nations, were of one way as well as of one heart. I know that I desire it sincerely. But I verily believe that when God shall accomplish it, it will be the *effect* of love, and not the *cause* of love. There is not a greater vanity in the world than to drive men into a particular profession, and then suppose that love will be the necessary consequence of it; to think that if, by sharp rebukes, by cutting, bitter expres-

[1] Works, Ed. Russell, xix. 571.

sions, they can drive men into such and such practices, love will certainly ensue." These are golden words, as true now as in Owen's troublous day.

Owen had his own scheme of comprehension. In his Tract on Union among Protestants (1680) he outlines a plan of a Larger Church of England by law established, which would include all dissenters, but exclude all Romanists. As a doctrinal basis he would have the articles of the Church of England as explained in the public authorized writings of the Church in the days of Elizabeth and James, "before the inroad of novel opinions among us," to be subscribed, however, only by ministers. All spiritual affairs were to be left with the churches, and "outward rites and observances" which were not inconsistent with the supremacy of Protestantism were also to be left to the free determination of the churches.[1] But for such a large scheme as this England was not then ready. Owen anticipated the broad statesmanship of Arnold of Rugby.

Richard Baxter, the great English Prot-

[1] Works, Ed. Russell, xvii. 603, 604.

estant schoolman, was another prophet of Christian union. Living in a most stormy and trying age, when the spirit of faction ran high, when ecclesiastical fighting was the order of the day, he was the great peacemaker. He spoke in these terms of his disappointment over the result of the Westminster Assembly of Divines. Their scheme was not sufficiently comprehensive for him. "The Christian world, since the days of the apostles, has never seen a synod of more excellent divines than this and the synod of Dort. Yet highly as I honor the men I am not of their mind in every part of the government which they would have set up. Some words in their catechism I wish had been more clear, and, above all, I wish that the Parliament and their more skilful hand had done more than was done to heal our breaches, and had hit upon the right way, either to unite with the Episcopalians and Independents, or at least had pitched on terms that are fit for universal concord, and left all to come in upon those terms that would."[1] Baxter's

[1] Davies, Life of Richard Baxter, Lond. 1887, pp. 101, 102.

chief objection to the Westminster Assembly was (1) against their making presbyterial orders a matter of divine right. This, he saw, would form another separating barrier. Baxter was a Presbyterian, but would be now classed as a Low-Church Episcopalian. That is, he believed Episcopacy to be a convenient and very ancient form of polity, though without Scriptural authority. "As to fixed bishops of particular churches, that were superior in degree to presbyters, though I have nothing at all in Scripture for them, yet I saw that the reception of them was so very early and so very general, I thought it most improbable that it was contrary to the mind of the apostles."[1] Baxter would have had a modified presbyterial episcopate as a centre of union for all parties, and would have thrown overboard all "divine right" theories of the ministry as divisive and false. But more important still was his objection (2) to their doctrine of coercion. He saw that this would only accentuate Church divisions and embitter all parties. He says: "I disliked the course of some of the more rigid of them, grasping at a

[1] Autobiog., quoted in Davies, l. c., p. 104.

kind of secular power. They reproach the ministerial power, as if it were not worth a straw, unless the magistrate's sword enforce it. What then did the primitive Church for three hundred years? Till magistrates keep the sword themselves, and learn to deny it to every angry clergyman who would do his own work by it, and leave them to their own weapons, the Word and spiritual keys, and, *valeant quantum valere possunt*, the Church will never have unity and peace. I disliked also some of them that were not tender enough to dissenting brethren, but too much against liberty, as others were too much for it, and thought by votes and numbers to do that which love and reason would have done."[1] This is as noble a testimony for toleration as it is for Christian union.

Baxter wrote to John Howe, the illustrious chaplain to the Protector, in reply to Howe's statement that the Protector desired Church union. Baxter says: "The Lord Protector is noted as a man of a catholic spirit, desirous of the unity and peace of all the servants of Christ.

[1] Autobiog., quoted in Davies, l. c., p. 105.

We desire nothing in the world (at home) so much as the exercise and success of such a disposition; but more is to be done for union and peace. Would he, first, but take some healing principles into his own consideration; 2d, when he is satisfied in them, expose them to one or two leading men of each party (Episcopalian, Presbyterian, Congregational, Erastian, Anabaptist), and privately feel them, and get them to a consent; 3d, and then let them be printed, to see how they will relish (with the reasons annexed); 4th, and then let a free-chosen assembly be called to agree upon them, he would exceedingly oblige and endear all nations to him; and I am confident, as I live, that by God's blessing he may happily accomplish so much of this work, if he be willing, as shall settle us in much peace, and prevent and heal abundance of our dissensions." [1]

But Baxter had fallen on evil days. His scheme for a modified episcopacy and a modified liturgy which he presented as a basis of union to the Savoy Conference in 1661, after the Restoration, was re-

[1] Quoted by Davies, Life of Baxter, p. 175.

jected by the Episcopalian party, and their own scheme of a stiff episcopacy and the whole unadulterated liturgy, which has been the watchword of the Church of England ever since, was buttressed by the Act of Uniformity, and the most holy and learned ministers of the Church of Christ in England — Baxter among them — were thrown out of their parishes, and many of them left to perish in hunger, in exile, or in prison.

Some years before this, in 1653, however, Baxter had formed the Worcester Association as a practical exhibition of union. He describes it himself: —

"The main body of our Association were men that thought the Episcopal Presbyterians and Independents had each of them some good in which they excelled the other two parties, and each of them some mistakes; and that to select out of all three the best part, and leave the worst, was the most desirable (and ancient) form of government."[1]

We may close our account of Baxter's contribution to this history by his ringing

[1] Church Concord, Preface, London, 1691, quoted by Briggs, Barriers to Christian Union, in Presb. Rev. viii. 452.

appeal to come together on the one Christian basis of faith, hope, and charity.

"Why, sirs, have not Independents, Presbyterians, Episcopal, etc., one God, one Christ, one Spirit, one Creed, one Scripture, one hope of everlasting life? Are our disagreements so great that we may not live together in love, and close in fraternal union and unity? Are we not of one religion? Do we differ in fundamentals or substantials? Will not conscience worry us? Will not posterity curse us if by our divisions we betray the gospel into the hands of the enemies? And if by our mutual envyings and jealousies and perverse zeal for our several conceits, we should keep open the breach for all heresies and wickedness to enter, and make a prey for our own poor people's souls; Brethren, you see other bonds are loosed; Satan will make his advantage of these daises of licentiousness. Let us straiten the bond of Christian unity and love, and help each other against the powers of hell, and join our forces against one common enemy."[1]

As a probable outgrowth of Baxter's able pleas and efforts for union, a movement among the clergy in Cambridgeshire

[1] *Christian Concord*, London, 1653, p. 96, quoted by Briggs, *Presb. Rev.*, 1887, p. 454.

during the years 1656–1658 may be cited. Dissociated from any compulsory measures and based upon a purely voluntary principle, it reflects an earnest spirit, which in many souls longed and labored during a tempestuous period for spiritual unity and harmony. From a very interesting and detailed account[1] of the proceedings of this association of ministers we make a few selections illustrative of the purposes which brought them together: —

"Jan. 20: 1656: At a meeting at Cambridge it was upon the question resolved:

"1. That wee all meet monthlie, & every time wee will bee all present, unlesse a rationall account can bee given to the contrarie, & that wee will meet Feb. 3: 1656.

"2. That in our meetinges wee will keepe our selves close to our proper busines, not medling with the civill affaires of the com̄onwealth.

. . . . . .

"5. That wee all will agree to the same order & method in administration of ordinances even in circumstances as far as possibly wee can.

[1] For full account, see The English Historical Review, Oct., 1895, pp. 744-753, with introductory paragraph by Rev. H. W. P. Stevens.

"Feb. 3: 1656. Mr King of Fulmire moderator.

. . . . . .

"3. That wee determine as neere as wee can to promote an uniformitie in catechisinge.

"April 7: 1657.

"1. Whatsoever wee have doe or shall resolve upon wee agree to put in practice till publike authoritie shall settle some things more particularly.

. . . . . .

"All scandalous persons hereafter mentioned are to be suspended from ye sacrament of the lords supper.

. . . . . .

"Any person, father or mother, that shall consent to the marriage of theyr child to a papist or any parson that shall marry a papist. Any person that shall repayre for any advice to any wiche wizard or fortune teller.

"May 5: 1657.

"1. As to the article in the ordinance for scandall relating to those that repaire to Wiches Wizard & fortune tellers &c. It was this day advised that wee shall account all those guiltie of that scandall who repaire to any that are famed to bee such, though not convict by law.

"2. Also wee advise that they who use

spelles or charmes, or pretend to use them thereby to deceave others, shall bee accounted guiltie of scandall.

" June 2: 1657.

. . . . . .

"4. Wee judge it may bee convenient that the agreement of the Ministers of this Countie touching Catechising, private instructions of our people, & administration of sacraments bee in some way made publikely knowen to our people."

A very interesting movement was that to bring together the Gallican and English churches. But this must now be passed over. Lupton has just made it the subject of an instructive monograph.[1]

Robert Hall (d. 1831) was an earnest advocate of Christian union. His words are fully equal to those of the latest zealot in this matter. He says:—

" Nothing more abhorrent to the principles and maxims of the sacred oracles can be conceived than the idea of a plurality of true churches, neither in actual communion with each other, nor in the capacity for such communion. Though this rending of the seamless

[1] Archbishop Wake and the Project of Union (1717-1720) Between the Gallican and Anglican Churches. London, 1896.

coat of our Saviour, this schism in the members of his mystical body, is by far the greatest calamity which has befallen the Christian interest, and one of the most fatal effects of the great apostasy foretold by the sacred penman, we have been so long familiarized to it, as to be scarcely sensible of its enormity; nor does it excite suspicion or concern in any degree proportioned to what would be felt by one who had contemplated the Church in the first ages. Christian societies regarding each other with the jealousies of rival empires, each trying to raise itself on the ruin of all the others, making extravagant boasts of superior purity, generally in exact proportion to their departures from it, and scarcely deigning to acknowledge the possibility of obtaining salvation out of their pale, is the odious and disgusting spectacle which modern Christendom presents. The evils which result from this state of division are incalculable. It supplies infidels with their most plausible topics of invective; it hardens the conscience of the irreligious; it weakens the hands of the good, impedes the efficacy of prayer, and is probably the principal obstruction to that ample effusion of the Spirit which is essential to the renovation of the world."[1]

[1] Works I. 289. See Princeton Ess., 2d Series, p. 237.

This passage reveals Hall far in advance of the general sentiment of his day.

A beautiful irenicon was that of an American lawyer of the Reformed Church, Abraham Van Dyke, Esq., who in 1836 published a book entitled, "Christian Union; or an Argument for the Abolition of Sects." It was dedicated to the Rev. David Abeel, a missionary of the Dutch Reformed Church in the East. It is an earnest and pious plea for Christian union. Van Dyke had also the faith to believe that such a union would in fact soon be realized. This was a more daring faith sixty years ago than now. He considers every objection, and modern discussion has added but little to his systematic and large-minded presentation.

The irenic proposals of Van Dyke met with serious opposition from two influential sources. One was the opposition of the Protestant Episcopal Bishop of Kentucky, Dr. B. B. Smith.[1] He welcomed the book as an evidence of dissatisfaction with the present position of Protestantism, but he had no faith in the peaceable and

[1] Review of Van Dyke's book in Literary and Theol. Rev. ed. by L. Woods, Jr., Sept. 1835.

catholic plans of Van Dyke. These plans he ridiculed by calling them simply an "agreement that Christians shall not bite and devour one another." On the contrary, said Bishop Smith, it is futile to talk about Christian union until all Christians are agreed in one outward form of church organization. "What sort of union," says Bishop Smith, "among the followers of Christ should be proposed? Shall they be called upon to unite in some way or another as they now stand divided; or are they bound to agree in one outward form of Christianity? For our part we most explicitly avow our conviction that every attempt to put a stop to the dissensions and subdivisions which distract the Church must forever prove futile, until Christians are agreed in one outward form of Christianity. To talk about union in feeling and spirit, whilst there is disunion in fact, is about as wise as to exhort those to love one another between whom occasion of deadly feud exists." Bishop Smith himself was a High Churchman. He considered "one of the grand mistakes of the Reformation a separation *from* the Church instead of reformation *in* the Church." This hostile reception of the Dutch Presbyterian layman's pacific propositions on the part of this prelate of the Protestant Episcopal Church was a distinct intimation on the part of that church that nothing could be considered on this subject unless the adoption of the Episcopal Church constitution was laid down as the first plank in the platform.

Another powerful voice lifted against the too hasty adoption of the peace propositions of Van Dyke was that of the " Princeton Review." In an article published in 1836 the Review, then conducted by its founder, Dr. Charles Hodge, expressed hearty sympathy with the aim and spirit of Van Dyke's book, but could not go so far as the enthusiastic author for these reasons : —

(1) Truth is greater than union. In such an amalgamation of Christians some would have to lay aside their convictions, or keep silent respecting them, and either course would be disloyalty to the God of truth. " Every attempt to reconcile differences among Christians which involves the relinquishment of truth, or a compromise with important corruption, either in doc-

trine or worship; or giving countenance to what is deemed an injurious departure from what Christ has commanded, is undoubtedly criminal and mischievous."

(2) Such an amalgamation of the churches, on the principle that their diversities in doctrine and order, as long as they do not affect the fundamentals of religion, are of little account, and ought not to permit the most intimate union, would discourage that "searching of the Scriptures" and that earnest "contending for the faith" which is expressly commanded as a Christian duty.

(3) But such union, even if attained without dishonest sacrifice, would do no good. It would not produce love, and without love it would be a curse. The nearer the Christian denominations come to each other, the more they would fight. This writer does indeed express the hope that all the Reformed churches in the United States holding the Presbyterian system will be united in organic union, and that some alive then (1836) would live to see the day, but he says that even such a union as that he would strenuously oppose, because the conditions of friend-

ship and love which would make the union a blessing did not then exist.

In conclusion this able writer lays down the following principles: —

1. All who profess the true religion in its essential characteristics belong to the Church catholic, and ought to be so regarded by all who believe that Christ is one and his religion one.

2. Concurrence in some outward form of Christianity is not essential to Christian union, or to the communion of saints.

3. Yet everything that tends to divide the body of Christ or its members from each other is sinful.

4. The day is coming, and is not far distant, when the people of God will be so united both in form and spirit that they will feel that they are one body in Christ, and every one members one of another.

5. A formal coalition of all sects into one body under one name would not necessarily be Christian union.

6. The spirit of sectarism must first be slain, and the spirit of charity become triumphant in every part of the Church.

7. Attempts to break down the barriers which now divide Christians before such

baptism of the spirit of love is given are of no use.

8. Those churches which stand aloof from other churches on grounds not supported by the Word of God are guilty of schism. This applies to the Roman and to the Episcopal churches.

9. There will be at length a pouring out of the Holy Spirit in a measure never known since Pentecost, which will prepare the world for a consummation devoutly to be wished, — the formal and real union of all Christians.[1]

It remains to speak of irenic movements in smaller sections of the Church.

There was first the effort to bring together the Presbyterian or moderate party in the Church of England and the Congregationalists. Baxter was one of a noble band who saw that underneath all differences there was a real unity.

"There is no such difference," said Thomas Hill, a Presbyterian, in 1645, "for aught I know, between the sober Independents and moderate Presbyterians, but if things were wisely managed, both

---

[1] See Princeton Essays, 2d Series, N. Y., 1847, pp. 236-258.

might be reconciled; and by the happy union of them both together, the Church of England might be a glorious church, and that without persecuting, banishing, or any such thing, which some mouths are too full of. I confess it is most desirable that confusion (that many people fear by Independency) might be prevented; and it is likewise desirable that the severity that some others fear by the rigor of presbytery might be hindered; therefore let us labor for a prudent love, and study to advance one happy accommodation." [1]

On the side of the Congregationalists Jeremiah Burroughs advanced these magnanimous sentiments. It is notable to see that the finest and highest of recent words for the universal peace of Protestant Christendom are but the echo of these proposals of the seventeenth century.

"Why should we not think it possible," says Burroughs, "for us to go along, close together in love and peace, though in some things our judgments be apparently different one from another? I will give you

---

[1] An Olive Branch of Peace and Accommodation. Lord Mayor's sermon, 1645. London, 1648. p. 38. Quoted by Briggs in Presbyterian Review, viii., 451.

who are scholars a sentence to write upon your study doors, as needful an one in these times as any; it is this: *Opinionum varietas, et opiniantium unitas non sunt ἀσύστατα*, Variety of opinions and unity of those that hold them may stand together. There hath been much ado to get us to agree; we laboured to get our opinions into one, but they will not come together. It may be in our endeavors for agreement we have begun at the wrong end. Let us try what we can do at the other end; it may be we shall have better success there. Let us labour to joyne our hearts, to engage our affections one to another; if we cannot be of one mind that we may agree, let us agree that we may be of one mind." [1]

In answer to this flag of truce the Presbyterian ministers of the Provincial Assembly of London in 1653 sent forth the following: —

" A fifth sort are our reverend brethren of the New and Old England of the Congregational way, who hold our churches to be true churches, and our ministers true minis-

---

[1] "Irenicum to the Lovers of Truth and Peace." London, 1645. p. 255. Briggs as above, p. 451.

ters, though they differ from us in some lesser things. We have been necessitated to fall upon some things, wherein they and we disagree, and have represented the reasons of our dissent. But we here profess that this disagreement shall not hinder us from any Christian accord with them in affection; that we can willingly write upon our study doors that motto which Mr. Jer. Burroughs (who a little before his death did ambitiously endeavour after union amongst brethren, as some of us can testifie) persuades all scholars unto: *opinionum varietas, et opiniantium unitas non sunt ἀσύστατα.* And that we shall be willing to entertain any sincere motion (as we have also formerly declared in our printed vindication), that shall farther a happy accommodation between us.

"The last sort are the moderate, godly Episcopal men, that hold ordination by presbyters to be lawful and valid; that a bishop and a presbyter are one and the same order of ministry, that are orthodox in doctrinal truth, and yet hold that the government of the Church by a perpetual moderatour is most agreeable to Scripture pattern. Though herein we differ from them, yet we are farre from thinking that this difference should hinder a happy union between them and us. Nay, we crave leave to profess to the world that it will never (as we humbly conceive) be well with England till there be an union endeavoured and affected between all those that are orthodox in doctrine though differing among themselves in some circumstances about Church government." [1]

Unhappily, the England of the seventeenth century was too stormy for the fruition of such lofty desires. But on this continent twenty-four years before the Presbyterian Assembly of London issued that remarkable paper, there had been realized exactly the union for which these men were praying. At Salem, in 1629, the Plymouth Congregational Church and the Salem Presbyterial-Episcopal Church were united in one blessed fellowship, — a happy omen for this continent.[2]

An important union movement of modern times was that which resulted in the union of the Lutheran and Reformed churches of Prussia, in 1817. So far back as 1720, Christoph Matthäus Pfaff, chan-

[1] *Jus Divinum Ministerii Evangelici.* London, 1653. Briggs, p. 451.
[2] Bacon, Genesis of the New England Churches, pp. 471–477. Faulkner, On the Early History of the New England Church, in Reformed Quarterly Review.

cellor of the University of Tübingen, who had been influenced by Pietism, proposed a union between these two churches in his "Alloquium Irenicum ad Protestantes." Their points of union in doctrine, he said, were far more important than their points of difference. His thesis found no favor. Even such conciliatory theologians as Weismann of Tübingen and Mosheim of Helmstädt opposed it. Forty years later another seed was dropped. Heumann of Göttingen, a Lutheran, wrote a treatise in which he defended the Reformed doctrine of the Supper, and asked why the two churches could not come together, the Reformed holding in abeyance their doctrine of predestination, and the Lutherans their doctrine of the Supper. In 1764 this pamphlet was brought out by Sack, after the author's death, and fell like a bombshell in grave and quiet Germany. Many Lutherans replied to it. Others considered it favorably.[1] At any rate it prepared the way for the determined effort of King Frederick William III., stimulated by the memories of the Reformation which came to him at its three

[1] Kurtz, Church Hist., Macpherson's tr., iii. 109–110.

hundredth anniversary, to bring together the two churches. On the 2d of May, 1817, he addressed a letter to Bishop Sack and Provost Hanstein, in which he said, "I expect from you propositions for the easiest and most appropriate manner of uniting the two slightly divergent confessions." But it was easier to say this than it was to bring about a union. However, after many conferences and concessions it was brought about in 1821 — its outward symbol being a new liturgy in the preparation of which the pious king himself took part; but which many, both Lutherans and Reformed, thought too Catholicizing in its tendencies. This objection, however, was partially obviated in a revised edition in 1829. The result of the union was that there existed in Prussia, Nassau, Baden, Rhenish Bavaria, Anhalt, and Hesse the United Evangelical State Church, with a common government and liturgy in which these parties abode peaceably together, namely, the Lutherans, and the Reformed — both parties holding to their peculiar doctrines, but not considering these as points of division and strife — and a real union party, which had abandoned in reality or in effect a belief in these doctrines. But it was a question whether this union has been a great benefit to the German Church. Brought about by the will of the king, not meeting any deep need or response in the hearts of the people, it naturally alienated those earnest souls who held firmly to the Confessions, to whom doctrinal loyalty and strictness of faith and denominational love were the life of their life. A church cannot afford to part with these. The men in whom the Lutheran tradition was a living reality remained out of the union, and the harsh measures of the king alienated multitudes. Steffens was deprived of his professorship and died in exile. Guericke, of Halle, ministered to a small company of Lutherans in his own house, and was for that deprived of his professorship. Many clergymen were imprisoned. After 1840 these harsh measures were intermitted, and the king consented to the formation of a Lutheran Church, which was constituted in 1841. Then there were three churches instead of two. And yet there was something noble in the thought of the Prussian king in consolidating the churches of his dominions, thus facing a

Catholic unity with a Protestant unity, and there was something catholic and liberal in the way in which this was carried out. Neither party was required to renounce any essential doctrines.[1]

An irenic movement which has affected the ecclesiastical life of Scotland, and thence of the world, was that which brought together the great churches, — the United Secession Church of Scotland and the smaller and yet influential church, the Relief Church.[2] The spirit of the Relief Church was eminently catholic. Its founder, Gillespie, had been trained by Doddridge, and he, Gillespie, could say, "I hold communion with all that visibly hold the Head, and with such only," a sentiment which reminds one of the famous declaration of his great contemporary, Wesley, who said, "I desire to form a league, offensive and defensive,

---

[1] Kurtz, Ch. Hist., Macpherson's tr. iii. 178 ff.; Hagenbach, Ch. Hist., 18th and 19th Cents., Hurst's tr., ii. 350 ff. For later separations, see Kurtz, iii. 280 ff.

[2] It is not necessary now to go into the story of the origin of these churches. Dr. William M. Taylor has given a very clear statement in his article on the United Presbyterian Church of Scotland in the Schaff-Herzog Encyclopædia, iii. 901 ff.

with every follower of Christ." In 1847 the union of these two churches was effected with great enthusiasm. The United Presbyterian Church of Scotland has been one of the most aggressive and spiritual churches of Scotland. In 1876 the congregations of this church in England united with the English Presbyterian Church, making the Presbyterian Church of England. In 1852 one of the Secession churches of Scotland — that in which Dr. Thomas McCrie was the leading light — united with the Free Church of Scotland, and in 1876 the Reformed Presbyterian [Cameronian] Church — or a large majority of it — also joined its fortunes with the Free Church. Although there have been strong counter currents driving the Scottish Christians apart, there have been also strong centripetal movements bringing them together. For ten years negotiations were carried on by the Free Church between herself and the Reformed, the United and the English, Presbyterian churches with a view to union. But a small minority threatened to secede from the Free Church if the project was carried through, and it was wisely abandoned.

The General Assembly of the Church of Scotland has formally approached every Presbyterian Church in Scotland with the expression of her " hearty willingness and desire to take all possible steps, consistent with the maintenance of an establishment of religion, to promote the union of such Churches." Her efforts have as yet proved fruitless, but we must echo the words of the Rev. Pearson McAdam Muir, in his admirable brief history of the Church of Scotland, that " it is hard to believe that it is impossible to find a basis of agreement on which, without abandonment of principle or compromise of honor on either side, the now opposing communions may take their stand, and thus avert a long, unhappy, and disgraceful strife." [1]

In speaking of Scotch Presbyterianism we naturally think of the daughter on this side of the water. In 1837 the Presbyterian Church of the United States was unfortunately broken into two divisions — commonly called the Old School and the New School. But it was impossible that churches having the same creed and dis-

---

[1] The Church of Scotland, Edinb. and N. Y. 1892, p. 94.

cipline and not divided by any profound sectional and political feeling could remain forever apart. A new generation came that knew but little and cared less about the old causes of strife. Churches and pastors united in the ordinary ways of fraternal intercourse. Then the mighty struggle for the Union baptized the northern churches into a oneness of feeling. Patriotism became the hand-maid of religion. Why should not the Church be one as the nation is one? In 1862 the Old School Assembly proposed a stated annual and friendly interchange of commissioners between the two General Assemblies. This was met by a hearty response in the friendliest spirit by the New School Assembly. At a meeting of the Old School General Assembly at Newark in 1864, a number of ministers and laymen met together to consider organic union. This non-official body adopted a statement in which, among other things, they said: —

"It is believed that the great majority in each branch sincerely receive and adopt the Confession of Faith, as containing the system of doctrine taught in the Holy Scriptures, and approve the same government and discipline. On this basis we may reunite, mutually regarding and treating the office-bearers and church courts of each branch as co-ordinate elements in the reconstruction. There are difficulties in the way of repairing the breaches of Zion, which must be met and overcome by well-considered methods, and in a spirit of forbearance and prudence. Reunion cannot be accomplished, nor is it to be desired without the restoration of a spirit of unity and fraternity. We believe this spirit exists and is constantly increasing. That which should first engage the attention of the friends of reunion should be to find out how far unity of sentiment and kindness of feeling prevail."

The same year at Dayton, Ohio, that great scholar and irenic spirit of whom not only Union Seminary but the whole American Church has reason to be proud, Dr. Henry B. Smith, as retiring Moderator of the New School Assembly, preached a sermon in which he presented the subject of organic union "with singular felicity and power." In 1866 both assemblies met at St. Louis. There they mingled together in religious worship and in the sacrament of the Lord's Supper. Nothing could withstand the spirit that made for fraternity.

The Old School Assembly passed resolutions looking toward organic union, and appointed a committee to act with a similar committee of the New School Assembly. It was a thrilling moment in the history of the Church of God when the Rev. Dr. Phineas D. Gurley, of Washington, and the Hon. Lincoln Clark, of Detroit, walked into the New School Assembly bearing these overtures. With equal cordiality and readiness the New School Church met the advances of the Old School brethren. In 1867 a plan for reunion was submitted by this committee to both assemblies for discussion during another year. At this juncture an ominous voice in dissent was heard. In the Princeton Review for July, 1867, Dr. Chas. Hodge objected to the plan on the ground that the New School Church does not now receive and never has received all the doctrines of the Calvinistic system in their integrity, and that, therefore, union would not only be inexpedient, but morally wrong. This was met by an article in the American Presbyterian Review for October, 1867, by Dr. Henry B. Smith, denying this charge, and attempting to prove that the sense in which the New School Church received the Confession was precisely that claimed as the true one by Dr. Hodge; viz., the Calvinistic or Reformed. Both articles were published in pamphlet form, and scattered far and wide, and both, says the late Dr. Wm. Adams, "tended to the same result,— the conviction of the substantial oneness of both bodies in the receiving and adopting the Confession of Faith in the true, honest, liberal, common-sense and Presbyterian significance of those words." The bases for reunion as amended were adopted by the assemblies in New York in May, 1869, and were submitted to the presbyteries. At an adjourned meeting of the two assemblies the next November in Pittsburg, the returns from the presbyteries showed an overwhelming majority in favor of reunion, and in May, 1870, the first reunited assembly met in Philadelphia amid the rejoicings of innumerable saints and the congratulations of sister churches all over the world.[1]

[1] Presbyterian Reunion Memorial Volume, N. Y. 1870, esp. pp. 246-406. This volume gives all the facts and documents, and selections from addresses, etc. See also J. F. Stearns, Historical Sketch of the Reunion, in the American Presbyterian Review, July, 1869.

Another great union movement is that which brought together all the Methodist churches in Canada. In 1873 there were six Methodist churches in Canada; the Wesleyan Methodist Church in the Eastern Provinces, the Wesleyan Methodist Church in Ontario and Quebec, — two churches historically and organically separate, — the Methodist New Connection Church in Canada, the Methodist Episcopal Church in Canada, the Primitive Methodist Church in Canada, and the Bible Christian Church. The note for the bringing together of these bodies was struck by Rev. Dr. E. H. Dewart, in 1870. In the fall of 1870 an informal meeting of representatives of different Methodist bodies was held at the house of the editor of the "Christian Guardian," Dr. Dewart, in Toronto. From the beginning this powerful journal threw the whole weight of its influence on this side. In 1873 a plan for union was adopted by the Wesleyan Methodist Conference of Upper and Lower Canada, by the New Connection Methodist Conference, and by the Wesleyan Methodist Conference of the Eastern Provinces. The first united General Conference was held in Toronto,

September, 1874, — the first time in history when laymen were accorded equal representation in the chief court of any large Methodist Church. The name chosen for the united Church was the Methodist Church of Canada. This irenic result was an object lesson which the other churches could not resist. The Ecumenical Conference in London in 1881 intensified the desire for union. In 1884 the Methodist Episcopal Church in Canada, the Bible Christian Church, and the Primitive Methodist Church in Canada, merged themselves into the larger Church. Thus, where there had been six, there was henceforth to be but one Methodist Church in Canada. A grand example has in this way been set for other Methodist churches to follow. England is looking in the same direction.[1]

It does not fall within our scope to treat the union movements in the Anglican, Greek, Old Catholic, and Roman churches, tending toward a union of one with another, or any one with all. This would form a most interesting chapter, but it would require more time than is accorded to this lecture.

[1] Centennial of Canadian Methodism, Toronto, 1891. This volume gives full historical information.

Irenic movements of great moment have been those which issued in the formation of the Evangelical Alliance in 1846; of the British and Foreign Bible Society in 1804; the American Bible Society in 1816; the proposals of the House of Bishops of the Protestant Episcopal Church in 1886, which were reaffirmed by the Pan-Anglican Council of Bishops at Lambeth Palace in 1888; the proposals of a more catholic type sent forth by the Congregational churches of the United States in 1895; the formation of the Brotherhood of Christian Unity, of which Theodore F. Seward, Esq., is the leading spirit, in 1893; and the formation of the League of Catholic Unity in 1895. These are all parts of a great and widespread movement which will not fail nor be discouraged until the churches of God are not only one in love and faith and hope, but one in a confederated, or united, or organic life. When the people on a certain vessel skirting the South American coast were dying of thirst and cried for water to those in a boat passing near by, the answer came back: "Throw down your buckets into the water." The sufferers were sailing in the mouth of the broad

Amazon without knowing it. The spirit of union is in the air we breathe, and throbs in the tides over which we float from the nineteenth century into the calmer and sweeter waters of the twentieth.

IV

THE
CHICAGO-LAMBETH ARTICLES

BY THE RIGHT REV. HENRY CODMAN POTTER,
D.D., LL.D.,

Bishop of New York

THE
CHICAGO-LAMBETH ARTICLES

THE invitation which brings me here this evening named as the topic for my consideration what are known as the Chicago-Lambeth Articles. Those articles, however, have formed the subject of discussions on both sides of the Atlantic for nearly ten years, and I should be a far bolder and more self-confident person than I am if I could hope to contribute to what has already been said in regard to them any very helpful or substantial word. More than this, it may be well for me to say at the outset, that the recent action, or rather non-action, of the Chief Council of the Protestant Episcopal Church with reference to such constitutional or canonical enactment as would make those articles more speedily or practically effective, may well discourage any one whose relations are such as mine from urging their consideration or pressing their acceptance upon others.

It would, indeed, be easy enough to answer to this last criticism, that any great movement advances usually by more or less unequal, or apparently unequal, steps. An idea is broached, a general statement is made, a basis of action is proposed, which to many earnest minds seems precisely what they have been waiting for. Over against them as they look out upon the future of some great interest or institution there is a situation which, in many of its most obvious aspects, is full of perplexity and peril. It cannot be denied, I think, that this is a widespread sentiment with those who love our common Master, and who desire the spread of his kingdom, as to-day they look out upon the manifold divisions of Christendom. A late issue of a leading foreign ecclesiastical journal publishes the names and the number of new sects that have come into existence and have been formally registered in Great Britain alone during the past year. I have not the record at hand, but there were at least some half-dozen of them, and they represent the strangest and most eccentric vagaries of belief and practice. I shall not rehearse them here; but one in reading them could not resist the exclamation, "Is this, after all, the only fruit of all our strivings after Christian unity? Is disintegration and not re-integration to be the history of all our efforts to unify the discordant voices that profess the faith of Jesus Christ?" And when one adds to this the fact to which I have just alluded, — that a communion which, by its synodical declarations, has taken a foremost place in the movement for the reunion of Christendom refuses, or seems to refuse, such particular action as in one especial aspect of it, at any rate, would appear to have promised for those declarations some practical force and efficacy, the situation becomes not alone anxious and perplexing, but also not a little discouraging.

For one, I am prepared unreservedly to admit the apparent force of such reasoning; but it must be qualified, I think, here as always, by the general consideration to which I have just referred. No great movement such as that for the reunion of Christendom is at all likely, any more than any other great movement which has to steer its way amid the ignorance, the prejudice, the ecclesiastical antipathies that are common to human nature, to go forward without considerable and frequent discouragements. We have to reckon with conscientious convictions, however ignorant; we have to reckon with selfish interests, however carefully disguised; and most of all, I think, we have to reckon with that quite unconscious pride of infallibility, of which Latin Christianity is not, it is to be feared, the sole and exclusive depositary. "The Reformation," says a large-minded thinker of our own generation,[1] "had rid itself of an ecclesiastical falsehood; it had not yet seen the scholastic root of much of the doctrinal system that it established. It put the idols of its schools in place of the idols of the altar. It had not yet learned that the kingdom of God is not a metaphysical notion; it had not yet learned tolerance of opinions and essential unity among differences. This spirit was the parent of its virtues and vices together. The Lutheran was conservative, intellec-

[1] Dr. Edward A. Washburn, Epochs in Church History, p. 91.

tual, but without sympathy with any outside his evangelical communion. Calvin was logician, scholar, hero; but he could banish Castalio or burn Servetus, like the *malleus hercticorum* of past time, and rule Geneva as if it were a cloister of Benedict. His spirit passed into his disciples; it created Puritans, brave, conscientious, pure, yet men who could, like Colonel Gardiner, look at an Arminian as Anti-Christ, and think a surplice a rag of unrighteousness." Undoubtedly, since those days the animosities of differing Christians have greatly softened, but it would be a " fond conceit " to imagine that they had ceased to exist. And, even if they had, there would still remain those other grounds of difference which represent profound conscientious convictions, — convictions which if they ever yield, must yield, not to the touch of sentiment, but to a vision, at once clearer and larger, of what is essential truth. It is because, whatever may be the discouragements of the hour, I believe in the growth of such a vision and of the influence and the temper that best serve to prepare the way for it, that, for one, I am persuaded that what is known as the Lambeth Declaration has not yet done its whole work for the cause of Christian unity; and that those who have welcomed it as a true irenicon amid the divisions of our modern Christianity have not been misled by an iridescent dream nor the *ignis fatuus* of an impossible theory. Let me name the reasons that lead me to this conviction.

I. And first among them I would put the deepening conviction among all Christian people of the evils of division. If what is known as the Chicago-Lambeth Declaration has had no other value, it will always be, I think, a cause for profound thankfulness on the part of those who were first of all concerned in it that it stands distinctly for that. Some of us can very well remember a mode of argument which was common enough among our fathers, and which went to show that the so-called divisions of Christendom were on the whole a distinct advantage to the cause of Christ and the growth of his kingdom among men. I do not hear that argument any more. Dismissing, if one chooses, what has been called the vulgar and sordid criticism of our ecclesiastical divisions which shows how they involve an enormous waste of men, and money, and resources of every sort, there still remain other and graver considerations concerning which I thank God there is now a far larger concurrence. The favorite image which likened the various sects and fellowships into which Christendom is divided to so many regiments or battalions in a great army, must needs face and explain, if it can, the widespread hostility of those battalions to each other. The fact, of which any one familiar with the history of smaller or larger communities may easily assure himself if he chooses, that quite as often as otherwise the growth of any given communion is simply at the expense of some other close beside it; — the further influence of a condition of things which issues too often in creating in the minds of Christian people an attitude of which a critical and somewhat thrifty balancing of the claims of rival fellowships is often a predominant characteristic, — the wretched heartburnings, rivalries, misrepresentations, and animosities which are often the most conspicuous fruits of our divided Christendom, — these are facts which we cannot longer deny and which we attempt in vain to disregard. As one consequence of them I think we must all be conscious of the existence of what may be called a kind of "competitive Christianity," in which the strife is not to "provoke one another to love and to good works," but to provide such superior "attractions" as are in danger, often, of turning the sanctuary into a place of more or less distinctly theatrical display, and the worship and the teaching into a practical exhibition of the shopkeepers' legend, "We study to please." What a pitiful travesty of the august offices of religion, and of the solemn business of the sacred ministry! And yet, there are those who do not hesitate to defend it as imperatively demanded by what they are wont to call "the exigencies of the situation." It is because of this, I am profoundly persuaded, that so many devout minds are turned to-day to consider that essential evil which is the source of such a condition of things, — the evil of our manifold divisions.

II. Again: there is yet another consideration that with many is even more influential to-day in the hopeful direction I have indicated. When one comes to read the story of the infant Church as he finds it told in the New Testament, he very soon becomes sensible of what I may call — using the word in the sense in which one uses it of a poem or a picture, — its tender and sympathetic atmosphere. There were divisions in the early Church as there were heresies and rivalries; but, brooding over all, and finding expression in utterances of singular love and devotion, in acts of rare and constant self-sacrifice, there was an atmosphere which revealed a common purpose, which prized the common fellowship, which strove for the common good. It breaks out in such expressions as those of the great apostle who, speaking of those others who preached Christ from motives more or less single or worthy, yet exclaims, "But every way Christ is preached, and therein I do rejoice, yea, and will rejoice." Have we ever considered how tremendous must have been the attractive power of this pervading sentiment of loving and self-effacing enthusiasm — of a spirit that could not forget that the whole was larger than any part, and that it was for the triumph of the whole that all alike were to strive? Here at last was something which put mere selfish gain, or success, or triumph in its rightful and inferior place. Here at last was something which thrilled the hearts of those whom it had taken captive with a love larger than their own race, or land, or family. Here was something which, speaking of the Fatherhood of God, made it easier for men to believe in it, because they saw that one of its chiefest fruits was the true brotherhood of man. How far our modern sectarianism has produced any such effect upon Christian disciples themselves, I will not undertake to say, — but how far that same temper of dissension, division, mutual hatreds and hostilities has been instrumental in discouraging the approaches and chilling the enthusiasm of people outside of any Christian fellowship is a matter concerning which I am persuaded thoughtful Christian people are not longer in any doubt. They see in it something that, now at length, must be reckoned with, and they are turning with a concern daily more eager and anxious to find, if they may, its remedy.

III. Yet another influence, which has been most graciously and powerfully at work among us in the interest of a reunited Christendom, has been the deeper and more intelligent study of the Holy Scriptures. There is no more favorite method with unbelief, when it would discredit the religion of Jesus Christ, than to point out how its disciples, differing as they do concerning questions which are, or which have been, claimed to be of the most vital importance, have been wont to appeal to the same Book, and often, strangely enough, to the same words in that Book. That meagre and superficial reading of the Sacred Writings which has dealt with them as one would deal with a fetish or a charm, — which has led one, for instance, to submit the gravest questions, in some moment of supreme perplexity, to the answer to be gotten out of the Bible by opening the volume at random, — this it must be owned, and that too often by those who ought to have been examples in another and more excellent way, has been a characteristic of men's use of Holy Scripture in all circumstances, and in none more frequently than in those which are concerned with matters of theological or ecclesiastical controversy. That the Bible should be treated as literature; that men should he scrupulously careful always to turn upon it those lights which come from a knowledge of the times in which, and the men by whom, it was written; that its right interpretation must depend among other things upon the growth of a language, the progress of a civilization, the influence of an environment; and that, until we have inquired concerning these, the last thing that we are warranted in doing concerning a certain text or book, or institution, is to dogmatize about it. This conclusion, which has dawned so late and slowly upon Christendom, is coming more and more, thank God, to be a dominant conviction. Whether or no there is a new spirit in the pulpit, there is a new situation in the pews. Never was there a generation in which, notwithstanding all the froth and frippery of our lighter literature, there was so large a proportion of thoughtful men — and of women too — who were reading and thinking and inquiring for themselves concerning Holy Scripture. I mentioned not long ago, in a quite promiscuous company, Canon Mozley's "Ruling Ideas of Early Ages," and I confess I was genuinely surprised to find how many of those present had both seen and read it. When we are making a clever argument for our little view of Apostolic Succession, or of Baptism by one mode alone, or of the primitive form of Church government, or of some fragmentary aspect of the doctrine of the Incarnation, it will be well for us to remember that, sitting in the pews there may easily be some quiet man or woman who watches our cheap and mechanical manipulation of isolated texts, or our utterly unscholarly reading of some disputed passage, with a silent surprise, in which humor and sorrow are mixed in equal proportions.

Such men and women are, though they know it not, the heralds of a new era. That era, however superstition, or ignorance, or inherited prejudices may hinder it, will bring with it a new and nobler conception of the office of the Holy Scriptures, and of the way in which men are to deal with them. And when it shall come, one of its best fruits will be that new and larger light in which will be set this whole subject of Christian unity. Heretofore we have magnified our differences; henceforward we shall rather magnify our agreements; and reading the story of the dawning life of the Church in the light of those various faiths and civilizations and philosophies amid which it came to have its beginning, we shall see how Catholic and not Anglican, or Roman, or Genevan, was its basis, and how heavenly and not earthly was its spirit.

IV. And this brings me to another consideration which demands our grateful recognition in connection with the subject of Christian unity, and that is what I may call the growth of the historic instinct. No one can review the origin of those various religious bodies, which have arisen since the Reformation, without recognizing how significantly they witness to an awakening of some of the deepest spiritual instincts in those who were responsible for their inception, and, no less, to a profound conviction that some one aspect of Christian faith or practice was, more than any other, or all others, essential to the integrity of the Christian fellowship. But from such a position the step was not always a long one to another and very different position, — a position which substantially disassociated them from other and no less essential characteristics of the Christian Faith and Order, and which thus, ere long, maimed that Faith and practically disowned that Order in the interest of a single dogma. In this aspect of it, the history of the disintegration of Christendom is at once startling and tragic. The historic Unity was openly and recklessly flouted. The historic Faith was at once narrowed and perverted; the historic Order, corrupt, tyrannical, grotesquely distorted often in its practical exhibitions, was disesteemed and finally disowned. And so there has come to pass the spectacle of a divided Christendom, of a household no longer at unity in itself, rent and torn with a thousand frivolous dissensions, a spectacle of blindness and self-will for the warning of all future generations. But along with such a condition of things, or rather as a consequence of it, there has come the awakening of another and very different spirit. That study of Holy Scripture, to which I have just referred, and along with it of the records of those times which followed most closely upon the days and the acts of the apostles, has been fruitful to our own generation as to none other that has preceded it. The historic method, which has been found so helpful in other departments of inquiry, has been invoked, as never before, in our own. I may not venture here to recite, even in the most superficial way, the story of its achievements, but I venture to think that the longer and more carefully they are studied in connection with the subject of Christian unity, the more abundantly will they vindicate the positions assumed in what are known among us as the Chicago-Lambeth Articles.

What, now, were these positions? Let me venture, at the risk of repeating what may be abundantly familiar to most of you, to recite not only the terms of the "Quadrilateral" itself (as for convenience it has been called), but those others by which it was introduced. It was in the General Convention of the Protestant Episcopal Church, in the year 1886, that the House of Bishops united in these words:

"*In pursuance of the action taken in* 1853 *for the healing of the divisions of Christians in our own land, and in* 1880 *for the protection and encouragement of those who had withdrawn from the Roman obedience, we here assembled in Council, assembled as Bishops of the Church of God, do hereby solemnly declare to all whom it may concern,* and especially to our fellow Christians of the different communions in this land, who, in their several spheres, have contended for the religion of Christ:

"(1) *Our earnest desire that the Saviour's Prayer 'that we all may be One' may, in its deepest and truest sense, be speedily fulfilled.*"

This plainly enough admits that whatever inner and spiritual unity among differing Christians might exist, that unity for which Christ prayed — unity "in its deepest and truest sense" — did not exist.

"(2) *That we believe that all who have been duly baptised with Water in the name of the Father, and of the Son, and of the Holy Ghost, are members of the Holy Catholic Church.*"

This no less clearly affirmed or implied that a sole and supreme claim to membership in the Holy Catholic Church could not be made by any one branch of that church, to the exclusion of any baptized person, even though not of its own fellowship.

"(3) *That in things of human choice, relating to modes of worship, and discipline, or to traditional customs, this Church is ready, in the spirit of love and humility, to forego all preferences of their own.*"

This indicates a clear recognition of the apostolic distinction between things of primitive and permanent appointment and things ἀδιάφορα.

"*(4) That this Church does not seek to absorb other Communions, but rather, co-operating with them on the basis of a common Faith and Order to discountenance schism, to heal the wounds of the Body of Christ, and to promote the charity which is the chief of Christian graces and the visible manifestation of Christ to the world.*"

These words explicitly recognize that there is such a thing as schism; but no less clearly point out that its remedy is not to be found in a narrow and mechanical uniformity. And then the Declaration proceeds: —

"*But, furthermore, we do hereby affirm that the Christian Unity now so earnestly desired by the Memorialists (i. e., those who had memorialized the General Convention on the subject of Christian Unity) can be restored only by the return of all Christian Communions to the principles of Unity exemplified by the undivided Catholic Church during the first ages of its existence; which principles we believe to be the substantial deposit of*

Christian faith and order committed by Christ and His Apostles to the Church unto the end of the world, and therefore incapable of compromise or surrender by those who have been ordained to be its stewards and trustees for the common and equal benefit of all men.

"As inherent parts of this sacred deposit, and therefore as essential to the restoration of unity among divided branches of Christendom, we count the following, to wit:—

"(I.) THE HOLY SCRIPTURES OF THE OLD AND NEW TESTAMENTS AS THE REVEALED WORD OF GOD.

"(II.) THE NICENE CREED AS THE SUFFICIENT STATEMENT OF THE CHRISTIAN FAITH.

"(III.) THE TWO SACRAMENTS,— BAPTISM AND THE SUPPER OF THE LORD,— MINISTERED WITH UNFAILING USE OF CHRIST'S WORDS OF INSTITUTION, AND OF THE ELEMENTS ORDAINED BY HIM.

"(IV.) THE HISTORIC EPISCOPATE, LOCALLY ADAPTED IN THE METHODS OF ITS ADMINISTRATION TO THE VARYING NEEDS OF THE NATIONS AND PEOPLES CALLED OF GOD INTO THE UNITY OF HIS CHURCH."

Now then it will be seen that the force and meaning of these several bases or conditions of Christian unity turn largely upon what is understood by the preliminary phrase "the principles of unity exemplified by the undivided Catholic Church during the first ages of its existence." It has been just at this point that the growth among us of what I have called the Historic Instinct has been of such great value, as it is destined to be, we have reason to believe, to an increasing degree. Scholars in increasing numbers have turned to the Holy Scriptures, to the writings of Clement of Rome, of Ignatius, of Polycarp, who all three had been disciples of one or the other of the apostles, and had been made bishops by them in various cities, — to the witness of Irenæus, Bishop of Lyons, of Clement of Alexandria, of Origen, Cyprian, Justin Martyr, and Tertullian, to the teaching of the Apostolic Canons, and of the councils of Nice, Constantinople, Ephesus, Chalcedon, Antioch, and Carthage, and have discovered running through them all a general *consensus* whose significance cannot be mistaken. "Though those to whom authority in the government of the Church was bequeathed had to make further arrangements from time to time to meet the exigencies of events, — the astonishing increase in number, the adaptation of the Church's mechanism to its rapidly multiplying requirements, the settlements of differences that arose, and the decreeing of fresh ordinances from time to time for the further preservation of order, the unity of the body, and the purity of the faith," — the significant fact is that those in such authority, as Kettlewell has pointed out, "scrupulously kept to the same lines as had originally been laid down and received by them; the essential and fundamental principles and character of the Constitution were strictly observed; and no departure from them was permitted. If any attempt were made to infringe upon them or to disregard the ordinances upon which the foundations of their government had been established it was the duty and charge of one and all to stand up for them and to resist any encroachment or violation."

No less clear has it been to the candid student of ecclesiastical history that this primitive unity in the maintenance of the rule and government of the primitive Church had pre-eminent reference to three things, — the due appointment of rulers, the due and cheerful submission of the governed, and loyalty to scriptural and apostolic doctrine, without additions or perversion. When the Christian Church began to lose these, she began to lose the secret alike of harmony and of strength. Her hour of weakness came when rival teachers and rival dogmas contended with one another for supremacy; and when, breaking with its historic past, Latin Christendom undertook to erect upon the ruins of primitive Christian unity the insolent structure of the papacy the moment of dissolution was at hand. We deplore to-day the divisions of Christendom, and rightly; but no such cleavage between primitive order and modern Christianity was ever made as was made when Rome usurped a place which her Lord had never given her, and so taught every feeblest and most self-willed sect in all the world how to read into the Word of God its own meaning, and into the order of his Church its own self-seeking way.

Our hope, nevertheless, I repeat, whether for her or for ourselves, is in the candid study of beginnings; and I do not see, in this connection, how any student of history can be long in doubt as to what its lesson is concerning that which has been the great source of all our differences, the communion of the Roman Obedience. "That body is indeed to many, many minds," as Dr. Edward Washburn has impressively phrased it "a source of vague terror, to many others a miracle of power which compels a reluctant admiration. It seems to stand, after all the battle of these centuries, as impregnable as ever; it covers this new world with churches; it plots new leagues in Europe; and while it has lost Italy, and its power is crippled in Austria, Spain, and France, it challenges the strength of Germany. It could compel obedience even in the face of an old Catholic secession; it draws its converts from Protestant England, and dreams of the triumph, there as everywhere, of Ultramontanism. But surely if we soberly read history we need not be disturbed by such facts. It is not strange that such a power survives. It lives first of all by its traditional hold on the religious faith and habit of a large part of Christendom. We are never to forget that the Protestant Reformation was confined almost wholly to those German or Saxon lands where there had been a freer revival of science and letters and a national life never so fettered by papal despotism. Nor is it strange that the old attachment to the Church of the past, the memories of the noblest age of scholars and saints, the Church entwined with all the faith and habit of the people, should remain. The Old Catholic movement is the best commentary on this fact. We cannot look save with love and reverence on men like Döllinger and Hyacinthe who could not, till the last, give up their ancient religion, but dreamed of a reformed papacy; and we must be content that such movements shall work themselves out in such sober ways as may bring reform without destruction. It may be long before Rome shall lose this power which it has by its antiquity, and its seeming unity. It lives as the mistletoe, which keeps its own green bloom by the sap it draws from the trunk, but strangles the gigantic oak at last. But again it has its life from the influence it exerts beyond its own communion over the minds of many in a time of religious quarrel and unbelief. It seems to rise before the eyes of doubting men as the only representative of the unbroken Church. Every age since the Reformation has seen the examples of conversion from Protestant ranks. We have seen it in our own day, in noble minds like Newman, seduced by the dream of Catholicity, and dismayed by the growth of religious freedom. It can blind the scholar by its pretended historic claims and dazzle the imaginative by the charm of its ritual. There is a compact strength in its organization which makes it far more effective than our free Protestantism. It has the drill of an ecclesiastical army. It has the might of an unscrupulous logic. . . . It proclaims the infallibility of one head; it allows no freedom of opinion; it utters its historic falsehoods with the voice of the Ecumenical Council; it knows no code of faith or morals save implicit obedience. There is in all this a power which overawes the world. Newman tells us in his *Apologia*, that, even in his unenlightened, evangelical youth, he fell into the habit, he knew not how, when he went into the dark of making the sign of the Cross. It was a pre-Roman instinct. And his passage into the Roman communion was just this. It was his magic charm in his intellectual dark, and it is the *Apologia* of almost all who have followed him. The Roman obedience was not a faith, but an escape from thought. And we need not therefore imagine that it is very soon to be extinguished. It may be long before it loses its hold upon the half instructed intelligence, the imaginative and the credulous worship of the world."

But we turn back from this essentially modern or mediæval conglomerate of audacity and superstition, and sectarian intolerance, to that clear and simple portraiture of the Catholic Church which is given to us in apostolic history, and we feel instinctively that, sooner or later, that simpler and nobler ideal is to be redeemed out of the rubbish and error of the past and to be the ruling force in that which shall be the Church of a glorious future! Least of all need we fear for the essential unity of the Church of God. "We must resist," as that brilliant essay upon the Latin age from which I have just quoted reminds us,[1] " the discords and the loose unbelief which now as always

[1] Washburn, Epochs in Church History, p. 74.

threaten us. We must maintain the symbols of our faith and the historic order of the Church. But we are never to forget that the unity which was destroyed in that Latin Church was one that cannot return. . . . I know no stranger book than the Irenicon of Dr. Pusey, in which, after proving with the wealth of learning that modern Rome has substituted Mariolatry for Christian worship, he proposes an alliance with it on the basis of Trent, as if the Mariolatry he exposes were not the very development of Trent." Rather than this " we want the unity that consists in an open Bible, a sound intelligence, a better learning, a reasonable faith. Our fathers bought it in the fires of Smithfield and baptized it in the baptism of their blood, and we will keep it forever. The strength of the Church lies in this, that it works with the forces of a Christian civilization." And the whole tendency of those forces is in the direction of the closer alliance of all Christian people, the steady elimination of the sources of mutual misapprehension, the frank recognition of excellencies in those from whom we are separated, and the economy of wasted forces, upon the basis of a mutual co-operation, which is mutually trustful, mutually respectful, and most of all mutually loving.

It is because the earliest days of Christian history are the days which teach us this lesson most clearly that, more and more, the better sentiment of our generation is turning back to study their story and to seek to recover their spirit.

V. Finally, I look with hopefulness to the coming of a day which shall bring with it a recovery of primitive unity and the building of a Christian fellowship at once Scriptural and comprehensive, upon some such basis as the Chicago-Lambeth Declaration, because of my profound faith in the mission to the whole world of a Christianity which is not Greek or Roman, Oriental or Italian, but Anglo-Saxon. I can readily anticipate at this point how some one may say, " But is not such an expectation an illustration of precisely the blunder upon which you have just been so freely commentating? You have told us that one reason why we may not look for the reunion of Christendom along the line of the Roman Obedience is because it stands for a type of Christianity which is not

Catholic but local, and what you have not told us church history has abundantly shown; viz., that the earliest divisions of Christendom came to pass not alone because of the strife of this or that branch of the Church of Christ for supremacy, but also because of that centrifugal force in all national churches which tended to drive them apart into merely national camps." Of this tendency it must be owned that the history of the Eastern Church is an impressive illustration. Its dominant type to-day is not Greek but Russian. Apart from the Russo-Greek Church the churches of the East have little life, little learning, little aggressive power. And no one who knows the East, and Russia also, can be insensible to the fact that in that mighty empire the features of a narrow and intolerant nationalism have overlaid those others which in the earlier history of the Eastern Church made it the witness of a primitive faith and of the apostolic temper. Yet these are the two great types of national Christianity to-day: the Latin, arrogant, intolerant, unscholarly; the Greek, narrow, slumbrous, and unaspiring. "Surely," it may be said, "the Church of the future, whatever may be its dominant characteristics, will be free from the tint and taint of any merely national characteristics."

But at this point there salute us certain significant facts which we cannot wholly ignore. One of them relates to what Dr. Bushnell called the out-populating power of Anglo-Saxon Christendom, especially since the days of the Reformation. The other day, in London, a civic corporation gave a dinner to the governor of the British Colony of Queensland. The banquet was co-incident with that explosion of American hostility to Great Britain to which I may not more particularly allude; and one of its most conspicuous guests was the Colonial Secretary of the English Government. In a speech made on that occasion Mr. Chamberlain alluded to the stress which had been laid in public criticisms of England's foreign policy upon what had been called the "isolation of England," and remarked, not, I apprehend, without a somewhat pardonable complacency: "The statement of our adversaries is quite true. England is an isolated power; but she has always thriven upon her isolation. She is without foreign alliances, but she has the devotion of all her children; and it may interest her friends in Germany [one can imagine the savage resentment with which the foolish young Emperor of Germany must have read the words], to know that the territory of the single British colony whose governor we are honoring to-night is three times as large as the whole German Empire; and that of such colonies Great Britain has to-night no less than seven," — in other words, that the Colonial Dominion, alone, of Great Britain is no less than twenty-one times as large as the whole Empire of Germany.

Now, then, have you ever stopped to consider what such a statement as that, made by a government official, scrupulously careful as to his facts, really means? Have we ever stopped to consider the larger question, — what that is which this amazing reproduction upon all sorts of foreign soils of the Anglo-Saxon really stands for? There is no fact, so far as my observation goes, so significant and yet so little appreciated in all our modern history as this. Think how much older the civilizations of the Latin races are than that of this complex type which for want of a better name we call the Anglo-Saxon race. Think of the history of the progress of Christian civilization, as compared with that which the English people have achieved. They were Spaniards who first came here, we say, and gave Christianity to the Western Hemisphere. What has become of Spanish Christianity in this northern continent, and what, as a moral, intellectual, or spiritual force, is it worth to-day in the southern? What impression has French civilization made upon Algeria, or Russian upon Turkey, or German or Italian upon Asia Minor or Africa? The donkey-boy who runs at your stirrup in the streets of Cairo speaks, next to Arabic, the tongue of the Greek or the Tuscan; but English ideas, aspirations, fashions, traditions, are those of which he knows the most. When the Queen of England walks abroad she leans, not upon one of her own sturdy Islanders, but upon the arm of an Indian servant from Bombay. Go to the country from which her favorite servant and subject comes. The old traditions, the old religions, the old prejudices and animosities are still there. But, penetrating them all in a silent and most singular way, are those other ideas and traditions which are transforming her courts of justice, which are recreating her social order, which, in one word, are making of the modern Anglo-Indian one of the most interesting and promising studies in the whole racial problem of the future. It is the same thing that we find in Africa, in Kamchatka, and in Japan. In this last nation the remarkable transformations which have come to pass have been the effects of a longing not for an English but for an American type of civilization, we are told. Yes, but what is the American type of civilization, after all, but the Anglo-Saxon type? We may change the scene, but the language, the laws, the literature, the traditions are substantially the same. And these illustrate, whether in the old world or the new, a remarkable quality of adaptation like which I do not hesitate to say there is nothing else in all the earth. It is a quality which will not be confined or shut in, and which has made the whole round world somehow conscious of the existence and sensitive to the touch of

Western civilization, as to none other that can be named.

Now, then, have you ever stopped to consider of what this is the prophecy in the religious history of the world? The basis of character in a nation is to be found in its moral ideas. The basis of moral ideas is to be found in a people's faith. It is true that in the great essentials of faith the nations of Christendom are one. But the grasp with which those same essentials are held, the hold which they have upon the common life of the people, the effects which they produce in conduct and character, are quite another matter. We have seen in other races and people than our own, however we may honor their fidelity to doctrinal formulas, a strange alienation of the popular life from the spell of their inner meaning. We have seen a divorce between precept and conduct so radical and so habitual as gave us a new sense of those tremendous words, "The letter killeth; it is the spirit that giveth life." We have seen the Word of God, as you may see it in the Coptic Church to-day, sealed up in a massive and richly decorated casket, but never by any chance opened and read for the teaching and guidance of the people. We have seen a system of morals such as that of Alfonso da Liguori accepted as the interpreter of duty for whole races of men. And all the while, too, we have seen the growing arrogance of a priesthood and the growing insensibility of the people. Do I need to set over against such a situation the story of Anglo-Saxon Christianity during the last three centuries? Not extravagantly did that gifted voice from which I have already quoted not long ago declare, "If we turn from the discords on the surface and ask what after all has been the fruit of this (later) Christianity on the real civilization of these ages, what for education, for a nobler philanthropy, for the social issues of a time that cares less for church politics than for the kingdom of Christ, — then I say, in spite of its rival sects, it is here that I recognize its meaning. . . . I look on the Church as a divine fabric, but its purpose is to educate the heart and life of mankind. If I go to those lands where the Reformation has sown its seed, if I compare with the intelligence, the private morality, the social virtue of these the conditions of the olden time, I need no better witness. Here, amidst all the strifes of doctrine or the divisions of sect, I know the real power of a religion which has renewed the conscience. I know that I shall be told of the loose growth of unbelief. But I cannot on this account blind my eyes to the reality. It was the worst feature of the so-called ages of faith that they obscured the moral sense of the world; there could be no awakening of the intelligent belief, of the self-governed will. It is so to-day, and it is the noblest gift of Anglo-Saxon Christianity to mankind that it has planted religion in the conscience, and that out of it has grown the harvest of its civilization." [1]

I know it will be said that all this may be true, but that it has very little to do with the power of such a Christianity to touch and transform the faith and life of other races than its own. But what is the larger significance of what is happening among peoples and faiths which, though Christian, have seemed most alien

[1] Dr. Ed. Washburn, Epochs in Church History, p. 100.

from our own? At Constantinople there is a college of the faith and order — so far as it is committed to any particular ecclesiastical order — which, unless I am mistaken, is that for which this seminary stands. It was my great privilege to visit it, not long ago, and to spend an evening under the roof of the rare man who is at the head of it. "We are not seeking," said Dr. Washburn, "to win these Roumanians, Armenians, Bulgarians and the rest, to abandon their own Christian fellowships. We are seeking to send them back, as graduates of this college, filled with a new spirit, to put fresh life into their old forms." And what have been the results of that noble and remarkable work? Some of them can best be appreciated when I say that to-day in Constantinople some five pulpits, if my recollection serves me, are filled with men who are graduates of Robert College, and who are in the orders of the Greek Church, — pulpits which for a generation or more previously had been wholly silent. When I add further that at the time these facts were communicated to me, nearly if not quite every member of the Cabinet of

Bulgaria was an *alumnus* of the same college, you will recognize, I think, not alone what a remarkable door has been opened to some of the best influences of Anglo-Saxon Christianity, but how remarkable would seem to be the adaptation of its whole temper and spirit in the direction of the awakening and unification of Eastern Christendom.

I can well understand how remote and visionary much of this will sound to one whose conception of Christian unity is that of a compact and symmetrical organization in which all local and national types shall somehow disappear under the super-imposition of hard and fast formulæ of dogma and usage. But of the two dreams I do not believe any thoughtful man can be in much doubt as to which is the more likely of fulfilment. The Chicago-Lambeth Articles are destined, I am confident, to survive the acrid criticism which is incapable of rising to an intelligent appreciation, whether of their letter or their spirit. More and more will it come to be recognized that they present not only a sentimental but an organic basis of union. More and more will it come to be recognized that what have been most freely faulted as their elements of weakness are really their elements of strength. They are the product of a race which, arrogant as it may sound to say so, has revealed itself to many men in many lands as having more than any other the future of Christendom in its hands. They may not bring about the result for which we all long, and to which, let me add, this honored institution and the men who are its strength and ornament have so nobly contributed, — to-day or to-morrow. But what of that? You and I, my brothers, can trust Him to whom, in the words of Bossuet, "the ages of men are moments of the disc of his eternity." And, meantime, the signs of His working are not wanting. "God is showing us as never before that the Church of his appointment, the Christian brotherhood of man, is needed in its fullest strength to meet the demands of a vast and confused civilization. The day is past when men of earnest thought are busied only or chiefly with the questions of church polity. It is what the gospel and the kingdom of Christ can do for the solution of the growing riddles of society, the inequality of caste, the purifying of the deep corruptions of our time, the overgrown luxury, the intricate diseases, physical and moral, the curse of serfdom, and (let me not be afraid to say it here!) the curse of war, the promotion of peace and of international union." Are we to solve these problems by sneering and railing at one another? The whole heart of Christendom cries out, in its better moments, against such a monstrous anomaly. May God hasten the day when, through your prayers and labors and sacrifices, and mine, it shall cease to be!

V

THE UNITY OF THE SPIRIT — A WORLD-WIDE NECESSITY

By the Rev. AMORY H. BRADFORD, D.D.
Pastor of the First Congregational Church, Montclair, N. J.

THE UNITY OF THE SPIRIT — A WORLD-WIDE NECESSITY.

ANGLICANS, Episcopalians, Roman Catholics, and all branches of the Christian Church which put emphasis upon the episcopate, begin arguments in favor of unity by emphasis upon the doctrine of the Church; while descendants of the Puritans emphasize the doctrine of the Spirit. Consequently the former favor Church unity, while the latter plead for Christian unity. A few Episcopalians teach that Christian unity must precede Church unity; while some descendants of the Puritans grant that Church unity must precede Christian unity. Into this discussion we are not led by our subject. I pause only to observe that, in the sense in which Paul used it, the saying "first that which is natural, and afterward that which is spiritual" contains a profound truth, and yet there is another truth still more profound. The basis of the natural is the spiritual. A more exact statement of what Paul meant would be, first, the spiritual; then the spiritual in its manifestation through the natural; then the spiritual freed from the limitation of the natural. Behind all development is a spiritual force. The ideal of the Church will not be realized by its being united in one body, obedient to one human will, and moving as one mass: the ideal of the Church will be realized when its members are harmonious, not because in one organization, but because filled with one spirit. The only power which really can unify is spirit. Unity which is not first spiritual is only formal, has no vitality, and cannot endure. It is our duty to pray and work not only for Christian unity, but also for the unity of the Church of Christ; but in my opinion that object will not result from Lambeth "Quadrilaterals," National Council Articles, or any other purely mechanical devices. Such declarations may help the cause by stimulating discussion, and they may hinder it by obscuring the real question at issue. Something vital and vitalizing is required. The one Church will be an organism, intensely alive, and an organism is never made; it always grows. In this case the order must be, first the spiritual, and afterward the natural or visible. This large and complex problem has many factors, only a few of which we can hope even to mention.

I. The student of current events cannot fail to have been impressed by the movement toward unity evident in all the world. For centuries the trend of things was toward individualism. That has not lost momentum, but it is now met by a coördinate movement toward unity. The desire for a united Church is one manifestation of a growing longing for a united world, and that united world is beginning to take shape in our time. The most remarkable fact in contemporary history is the progress which the nations have already made toward what we might call a "United States of the World" if it had not already been named "the Kingdom of God." The idea of the unity of all nations is no idle dream.

There is a movement among groups of nations toward a limited unity. The many German kingdoms have been merged in one German Empire; the petty Italian states, ruled by miniature sovereigns, have given place to "United Italy;" the prophetic statesmen of Great Britain anticipate imperial federation which may bind the British Islands, Canada, British Columbia, Australia, New Zealand, and South Africa in a closely articulated empire, with common language, history, religion, which will move together in all imperial projects. Russia is slowly but surely reaching her arms around nearly the whole of Asia, and when the Siberian railway is completed, Persia, and possibly even China, will be subject to the Northern autocrat. Among nations the word of the hour is unity.

This movement is more impressive when it is studied somewhat in detail. Armies and navies are glaring at each other as if eager to fight, but no one dares to begin. In the meantime railways are shortened; trains fly faster; steamers increase in speed; the attractions of travel are multiplying; trips around the globe are being exploited, and more people know the world well than formerly had a smattering of information about one land. The first Atlantic cable was laid easily within my memory; now there are many on that ocean, and many projected for the Pacific. All lands are open to travel and business.

But the movement of travel and commerce is less significant than that of thought. The same books are read in all lands. A Japanese who has never been abroad will talk to you of Hegel and Matthew Arnold, of Tennyson and Herbert Spencer, of Beecher and Brooks, as if all were natives of Japan. Morning papers in Tokyo and Shanghai have much the same contents as those of London and New York; while great European and American dailies have correspondents in the East. Occidental scholars are studying the religions and literature of the Orient, as scholars in the East the religion and literature of the Occident.

These facts show that in spite of selfish statesmanship the interests of one nation are the interests of all. We are in the midst of what may be termed a worldwide movement. The Church is affected by the Zeit-geist — which in this instance is the Holy Spirit.

II. Our second proposition has the force of an axiom: a united world cannot be conquered by a divided Church. The world is becoming one, and the Church must therefore close its ranks. It will be well here to observe some things not included in this idea of a united world. A common language may not immediately result, but it is evident that as travel increases and the volume of business expands, there must be a popular medium for international intercourse.

History and traditions cannot be changed, and they make the obliteration of individualities impossible. Unity does not necessitate sameness, but rather the blending of things that differ. The path by which various peoples have advanced is dear to them; they cherish the memories of the great souls who have led them to victory, and do not forget that they have risen on the sufferings of heroes long dead. To take reverence for ancestry from the Japanese or Chinese would be more difficult than to make the leopard change his spots. Without looking for impossibilities, I affirm that the nations are actually, though not always consciously, beginning to anticipate a common future. They are like streams which have risen in many countries gradually nearing one another; by and by they will meet and swell a mighty river; the river will be one, and yet from it will run silver lines to many and far distant mountain springs.

Again, there is no likelihood of radical changes in what may be called racial nature. Men will get together, but those subtile differences of temperament and character which, in large measure, are the results of physical environment will remain. The unity of the world will affect neither the climate nor the configuration of various lands: consequently while widely separated nations may come together, it will not be into uniformity and monotony, but into the use of what belongs to the individual nation for the common good. The highlands will still breed heroes, while the lowlands will raise agricultural and commercial peoples; but railways and telegraphs will bring highlands and lowlands so near to one another that their interests will be the same, and each be seen to be necessary to the other.

Since individualities will not be destroyed by this unity, it follows, of course, that intellectual processes will not be materially altered. In the same land now one is a poet and another a philosopher, and in the drawing together of the races men will differ intellectually as in the past. The German and the Chinaman will be slow and steady; the Frenchman and the Japanese quick and mercurial. The difference between the mental and moral characteristics of nations is as great as that between their physical characteristics. Steamers and telegraphs will affect a man's intellectual faculties no more than the color of his face or the texture of his hair. Each nation will modify every other, and the common thought will be different from what it is now precisely because what one people think all people will think; but the intellectual faculty, which is largely the product of ancestry and environment, will remain practically as at present. If the faculty is not changed, the processes, which are the paths along which the faculty moves, will not be greatly changed.

While slowly but surely the people of the world are being united; while the movement must be accelerated, it is not toward dead and barren uniformity, but toward such a union as will allow full play to individuality and yet blend all in one great harmony. In other words, among nations there is a growing spiritual unity. If the Church would reach all classes, and breathe into them divine inspiration, it must be a united Church. While Providence is promoting political unity, making men see eye to eye, and desire the same things, it is folly for the Church to be divided into warring camps in which one does not recognize the other, and over which sometimes are raised hostile flags. A united world calls for a united Church, a Church of the spirit, in which there may be many and great differences, but in which the differences will all be dominated by a mighty and magnificent spiritual energy.

From this study of the movement of events and the call of Providence I turn to ask how far this superlative idea is realized. I must grant that there is more real unity than facts at first would seem to indicate, and that what now exists is sure to grow and must not be overlooked. But my object is not to speak of what has been achieved so much as to place in clear relief the vast, and sometimes discouraging, task which is before all who believe in the kingdom of God.

1. The condition of that part of the world commonly called heathen. Until one has travelled extensively, and studied carefully the religious condition of the unevangelized nations, he has a faint conception of the smallness of the beginnings of Christianity, and no idea of how the Christian faith sometimes reacts against itself. This is seen in the rivalry to which it stimulates the non-Christian religions. Buddhism and Mohamedanism are lethargic, and content to be so, until inspired to activity by the presence of Christianity. Then they adopt its best methods, and fight it with its own weapons. From being mere names they become aggressive and persistent antagonists. It seems sometimes as if Christianity were hardly more than a ripple on an infinite ocean. In Japan less than one-fourth of one per cent. of the nearly 42,000,000 of people are even nominally Christian. In China the proportion is not so large. In the Sandwich Islands the natives, though in touch with the Church and

its influences, seem to be dying out or largely returning to barbarism. Of the 400,000,000 in India an insignificant proportion of natives acknowledge the sway of the Christ. There is a bright side in the heroism of the missionaries, who are persistent, brave, confident of victory; but the cause has not progressed far enough to justify the slightest division among the workers. And yet in every non-Christian land there is multiplicity of sects. A Wesleyan bishop from Canada is reported to have found in one small town in Japan four different branches of the Methodist Church, requiring the presence at stated in-intervals of three or four different bishops from America and Great Britain. The report is credible. I have seen in one place after another in that country Presbyterians, Baptists, Anglicans, American Episcopalians, Methodists North and South, Wesleyans from Canada, confusing natives by different names, insisting on insignificant details of their own organizations, when an impression had hardly been made on surrounding heathenism. What do Japanese or Chinese care about the Historic Episcopate? What must be the effect on a converted Buddhist when he is told that, because he has not been immersed, he must not partake of the Supper of the Lord with a saintly heroine whose name is known from one end of Japan to the other for unparalleled devotion in the hospitals, and who, perhaps, saved his life when he was wounded? Multiplicity of Christian sects confuse those who feel the inadequacy of the old religions, and who have dared to hope that our Master might be indeed the Desire of all Nations. In the face of a united, defiant, and often blatant heathenism we present a divided camp. If it be said that there are sects among the ethnic religions, I reply: Yes, but they all make common cause against Christianity. Cursory travel through a country might not show this fact, but when one has studied the life of the people and come to understand its inner forces, he finds that the multitudes are confused and confounded because Christ seems to be divided.

There is another side to this question. Those who stand between the various missionary and philanthropic causes pleading for assistance and the givers in the churches must ask themselves whether this tide of entreaty will ever ebb. I confess I think it is time that this subject was faced. Is not the Christian Church being constantly and persistently invaded by agents in the interests of so-called charities to the peril both of the Church and individual souls? The plea for humanity was never more urgent, but is there not baneful and wicked extravagance in the way benevolences and missions are administered? Have we a right to go to our people and urge sacrifice in giving when those sacrifices are not in behalf of the kingdom of God, but that senseless and wicked divisions in the Church may be continued? With co-operation the missionary service of the world might be administered by a much smaller number of executive officers at vastly diminished expense. In order that those who are in darkness may be told of Christ every Christian will gladly deny himself; but if the effort is to supplant one denomination by another we may well inquire if extravagance and injustice have not already been carried too far.

These facts, then, meet us as we study the field occupied by the foreign missionary societies: the work is altogether out of proportion to the number of missionaries; and there is poor economy in the use of both men and means. Only to intrepid faith is there hope that those millions will ever be greatly affected by the gospel. It is opposed not only by natural wickedness, but by the organized aggressiveness of older faiths, which cannot be displaced without a determined struggle. Workers in foreign fields are opposed by corrupt conditions which have behind them the sanction of centuries; philosophical theories which regard the faith of Christians as absurd; governments which look with suspicion upon everything which teaches men to think. The contest — except for those who have faith in God — is unequal and hopeless. Yet, in spite of obstacles, young men and maidens, with courage and enthusiasm, are volunteering for forlorn hopes in numbers greater than ever. They are taking up their work, and dying in the service as if victory were at hand. In view of these facts, is it not time for the ranks to be closed, and for everything which prevents co-operation to be swept from the Church, no matter who suffers?

2. When we turn from the foreign to

the home field, to the work which remains on frontiers and in great cities, we find a problem equally complicated. A pastor who had spent years in India said to a friend considering a call to London: "Come to London; it is the greatest missionary field in the world. I know, for I have spent years on mission ground." In many localities the cities are relapsing into barbarism. Forces are working toward heathenism here as fast as in Central Africa. Selfishness is organized and belligerent. It opposes the Church at every step. It uses consummate ability in the degeneration of the State, in the exaltation of unworthy ideals of patriotism, and in its appeals to passion to embroil nations. Underneath these evils are others more elusive but not less perilous. The multiplication of divorces tells a sad story. The home is being undermined. The young are being polluted by influences alert and obstinate because impelled by the prospect of financial gain. Opposed to those agencies of selfishness are spiritual forces working for the redemption of society; but closer study shows that those through whom the Spirit must act are not organized, often do not co-operate, and not infrequently antagonize one another. In small towns there may be a dozen different churches with seldom a union meeting, where a union communion service is impossible, and where there is not the slightest consultation as to how the kingdom of God may be best promoted. This is no exaggeration. When were the representatives of all the various churches in New York gathered for conference concerning the things all have in common? I venture to say that never in its history was such a meeting held. Here and there are hints of what might be. The "East Side Workers" is a suggestion of better things. But were Protestants and Roman Catholics, Episcopalians and Baptists, Methodists and Presbyterians, Unitarians and Universalists, by their leaders ever in honest conference where differences were sunk and only this question at the front, — How may those who bear the name of Christ best do the work of Christ in this great city? But you ask, "How could those who differ widely work in harmony?" I reply by asking, Are there no common foes for all to fight? Churches are built where churches are not needed, and localities where churches are needed left desolate because the interests of the denomination are put above those of the kingdom. The missionary treasuries are empty and disgracefully in debt. I believe with proper economy in the administration of foreign and home work, without regard to denomination, there would be money enough. It is not the hard times alone which have emptied the treasuries; it is the selfish way in which great trusts are administered. The disaster is not less because the selfishness is not intentional. The trouble is that beneath what we call principle, in many instances, is far more of competition than of the spirit of Christ.

In this connection consider the debts of the missionary societies as they were but a few weeks ago.[1] The Congregational Foreign Board, $115,000; its Home Board, $77,000; the Methodist Board for Home and Foreign Work, over $209,000; the Presbyterian Boards for Home and Foreign Work, about $306,000; the Baptist Board for Home Missions, $190,000.

[1] These figures are taken from The Independent of March 5, 1896.

When the pressure of debt was heaviest, what did our various societies do? Instead of getting together and inquiring how missions as a whole might be more economically administered, they did two things: they reduced the salaries of the missionaries and the appropriations for the work — already too small; and they increased the number of agents whose business it is to appeal to already overburdened churches for increased subscriptions. There have been progress at home and splendid victories abroad, because truth makes itself felt in spite of the methods by which its interests are often promoted, but it is time that the facts which thus far have been stated were faced and given Christian consideration.

The question now arises, What shall be done? It is folly to describe symptoms unless remedies may be suggested. I am addressing a theological seminary, and that leads me to say that the first thing for a Christian man to do is to set himself like a flint against the multiplication or perpetuation of divisions and strife. It is not within my province at this time to enter more into detail. Fortunately the mighty movement throughout the world in behalf of the unity of man is making itself felt, not only among nations, but also among denominations, and in that we find the best answer to our inquiry. As the world is becoming one the Church must become one. The cry for a united Church is as strong and persistent as that for a united world. It has come none too soon. Against heathenism at home and abroad the momentum of spiritual unity must be hurled. Not more missionaries, but more force behind those already in the field! Not more places for preaching, but a mightier power behind those already in the pulpit! One missionary may do little; a thousand in perfect harmony will not easily be resisted. "Ah! but," you say, "do you plead for a mass like the Salvation Army, in which individualities are subject to order and law? Would you have the churches of the world under the direction of one man who should represent Christ on the earth? We had better all become Roman Catholics at once. It will make little difference who is the Pope." Shall we have one great Salvation Army? No! The more compact the organization and the more inflexible the rules, the surer will be the tendency for individuals to fly off on tangents of their own. A Salvation Army for the world under one man might work if that man were perfect, but no such man is in sight, and never has been. As men are now constituted, such unity is neither possible nor desirable. But what shall we have? I plead not for uniformity of organization, but for the unity of the spirit — the only unity possible for personalities. What do I mean by that? Exactly what our Master meant when he prayed for his disciples, "That they all may be one; as thou, Father, art in me, and I in thee, that they also may be one in us." When all are inspired by the spirit of Christ there will be unity of purpose, unity of effort, and harmony of temper. As fast as men are possessed by that spirit difficulties and discords will disappear. Let me give you a few illustrations of what has resulted from its absence.

When Dr. Pentecost went to India in 1891, he saw that co-operation was indispensable to the success of his mission. He appealed to members of various churches, among others to priests of the Anglican communion and to the bishop. In reply he was told by the latter that he could not be recognized as a Christian preacher because he had not been episcopally ordained. When he suggested to one of the chaplains of the bishop on a week day that it would be his pleasure to attend the cathedral on Sunday, and receive the communion, he was told that if he had not made his purpose known, stating that he was a Nonconformist, he might have done so, but now that he had made it known it was probable that permission would be refused. The matter was referred to the bishop, who answered that while he had no objection to him as a man, yet because he was an avowed Dissenter he could not allow him to receive the Lord's Supper; that it would have been allowed if he had not mentioned that he was a Dissenter — although that fact was well known before. There was the Christian name, and but little of the spirit of Christ.

For many years the American Board had had missions in Turkey. It had become familiar with the peculiarities of the field, and could work it most efficiently. There came from that country to the United States an erratic young man of brilliant ability. Against the advice of missionaries, he appealed to the American Board to help him in his studies, and his appeal was not granted. He then went to the Baptists; by them was educated; by them sent back to Turkey to found Baptist churches. He quickly ran his course and left the ministry; but an element of discord was introduced where there ought to have been harmony. The newspapers took up the matter, and controversy followed. Either the man was unworthy and ought not to have been approved by either society, and so the Baptists were more anxious about denomination than about the kingdom; or the Congregationalists were mistaken and ought to have encouraged the man whom they refused. However the blame may be distributed, there was division, and the work was hindered. There was not the unity of the spirit.

Presbyterian missionaries had long been doing superb service in Persia. Elsewhere were territories untouched by the gospel. Why did not the Society for the Propagation of the Gospel in Foreign Lands seek some unoccupied field? Instead, with arrogance and exclusiveness, their missionaries went to Persia, refused fellowship to the men who had opened it to Christianity, and by their action said that those who had learned about Christ from Dissenters were as much in need of missionaries as if they had never heard of Him. Thus the Persians were taught a religion of strife. Such assumption would make one's blood boil were it not at once pitiful and laughable. There was little of the spirit of Christ in the councils of that society when its action made that controversy possible.

In many of the cities in unchristian lands where there is an English-speaking population union churches have been formed, as in Honolulu, Yokohama, Tokyo, and Kobe. In all cities that I know, except Honolulu, there are barely people enough to make one small congregation, and in Honolulu only enough for one fair-sized congregation. Public services can be maintained only by concerted action and mutual concession. But what are the facts? In Honolulu, first the Episcopal Church introduced the wedge of division; then the Methodists drove it a little deeper; and now certain Baptists are trying to induce the only persons whom they recognize as having been baptized to drive it deeper yet, and are so blind that they do not seem to see that the iron of that wedge is going straight into the body of Christ. At Kobe the Union Church is small, seating barely two hundred people, and never more than half full. By an amicable arrangement one denomination has used the building one Sunday and another the next, and many persons have attended both services. That plan is now disturbed. Again the wedge of discord is being driven into the body of Christ. The sad fact is that the sects in those lands are not so many companies fighting a common foe, but starving societies competing for the patronage of a few resident foreigners, while heathenism captures more than half of the young men who go there as Christians. And yet missionary societies urge the people at home to give more liberally, that the good work of perpetuating rivalries may go on. An eminent pastor of this city recently went around the world, and returned with the sage remark, that the cure for the retrograde movement in the Hawaiian Islands would be the introduction of another denomination. And he lives to repeat his folly. I envy not the man who can go into a union church in a foreign city and raise a sectarian slogan. There is a judgment day for such persons. What is needed is the spirit of Christ — that is all.

Other illustrations are unnecessary. The story of Japan, Uganda, and India is well known. Despair of missions and of Christianity would be inevitable were it not for the prophetic souls who behind abuses discern the Providence of God making even human folly to praise him. But the fact that God overrules never justifies evil on the part of individuals.

The foreign field is full of discouragements, inconsistencies, losses, scandals, not because denominations exist, but because they exist so largely for the sake of themselves. When there is spiritual unity, only such denominations will enter foreign fields as are needed, and conference and co-operation will displace division. I admire the enthusiasm of "the student-volunteers," but about half of their energy will be lost because the effect of a blow is in proportion as the force behind it is massed. Send those men out to work together, and the effect will be sublime; send them out to be sacrificed to sectarianism, and the spectacle will be a shame.

I am not so foolish as to think that denominations serve no good purpose. When I find one class of people so narrow that they have no place for men whose minds are open to receive the fullest light on all the problems of religion, I rejoice that they can be in a little coterie by themselves, and hope they enjoy their company; when I hear others say that they are not willing to work with this evangelist or that, because, even though the Lord approves him, they cannot, I do not waste tears over the fact that we are not compelled to keep step to their music; when I find people who do not believe in social settlements, in institutional churches, in saving men except according to prescribed methods, — who, apparently, would rather the masses were lost than reached in unofficial ways, — I am thankful that they can have a nice and proper fold all to themselves, and I do not care much how high they build their fences. Such societies are good places in which to keep and discipline those small souls who do not appreciate our Saviour's intercessory prayer.

The Lord has had to endure many things because of the hardness of men's hearts, and evidently He will yet have to endure much more. Denominations in the past have served a good purpose, no doubt, and cannot be dispensed with yet; but they can and ought to be made the agents of the Spirit of God, rather than obstacles in the way of the kingdom.

Before the division in the Church can be expected to give place to the world-embracing unity for which we devoutly pray, there must be harmony among denominations. The better condition will follow the proper use of what we already possess. The first thing to seek, therefore, is unity of the spirit; with that we shall realize unity of organization as soon as it is desirable. Concerning unity of the spirit I observe: —

I. It is never the result of mechanical contrivance. All the bishops ever ordained cannot impart spirit. A million hands on a man's head may leave him without the unction from above. There is only one place whence that can come, — from the Holy One. Lambeth Conferences and General Assemblies might sit until the Judgment, and never show His presence.

We begin at the wrong end when we ask, How may we make Christendom one? When all who bear Christ's name have received the divine life they will be one. We must stop asking how we may have a united church, and humble ourselves for a baptism of power: then the united Church will take care of itself.

II. Until there is unity of spirit, unity of form will be worse than useless. If men are not agreed, no good can come from welding them together. Compel the Puritan to worship like an Anglican, and the Anglican to worship like a Quaker, and what will result? Make the Church a gigantic organization with numberless bishops, one being supreme, whatever the name, and there may be one body, but there will be no life, no divine fire. When there is unity of spirit, unity of form may be desirable, and not until then.

III. When there is unity of spirit, essential unity of organization will follow of necessity. Spirit organizes its own body. Our Republic is the body which the free spirit of the American people has organized for itself. You may build a box around death, and the box will last until it, too, decays; but if you build anything around life, it will be broken in pieces by growth. There is a divided Christendom, because those called Christian are without the divine life. Where the spirit is, there will be essential unity. Nature is the garment of spirit. I love to observe the variety of manifestation which the spirit assumes in the physical creation,—in flowers, in forests, in grasses, in ferns, in fishes, in birds, in all the races of man, in all forms of matter, so that there is a veritable universe. The Church may assume as many different forms as the creation, but with the spirit indwelling it will always be a universe. Let the spirit of God organize its own body.

IV. Only as there is spiritual unity can the kingdom of God be advanced either at home or abroad. The kingdom is the form which the spirit assumes. It was Jesus Christ, because the spirit was in him; today it is all in whom the spirit dwells. What is needed is that measure of coöperation which shall prevent division of energy; make lack of comity impossible; never allow the building of churches, the sending of missionaries, the spending of money for sectarian purposes. Denominations do not need to go, if the Spirit always controls; and yet I believe as we now know them they will go; at least there will be between them conference and mutual service, and never rivalry and ambition. When will the kingdom come? Not until the heathen see more of Christ and less of human mechanisms; and the work at home will fail except all branches of the Church, for practical purposes, are in perfect harmony. Before that day dawns, what an amount of rubbish must be swept away! What selfishness and conceit masquerading in garments of loyalty to conviction must be unmasked! World-wide movements require cosmic energy, and cosmic energy is the spirit which unifies and uses nationalities and individualities, rituals and creeds, for the kingdom of God.

V. But suppose we have this spirit, so that the prayer of Jesus is a reality, and we are one even as he and the Father are one — what then? Will all be realized? By no means. The kingdom grows. The way of the spirit is the way of life, and that is a mystery. The course which it will pursue no analysis can follow; but what some of the results will be are not difficult to determine.

Where there is unity of spirit, there will be generous recognition of every Christian, without regard to the name he bears or the creed to which he subscribes. Christianity being a thing of the spirit is discovered by the spirit. Those whom God has approved, need no certification of human official. Heart answers to heart. Those who have the spirit always recognize the spiritual.

Where there is unity of the spirit, there will be real fellowship. Church buildings will belong to the common Lord, and to his people; the Table of the Lord will not be held to be the property of one sect, but the right of all God's children. If an ecclesiastical rule keeps two ministers from exchanging pulpits, and they have the spirit, they will find some way to let the world see that rules can never sunder those whom God hath joined together.

Where there is unity of the spirit, there will be comity between denominations and individuals. No sect will think of intruding where it is not needed, but each denomination will help the one which can do the best work. On the foreign field and at home the inquiry will be, How may we manifest to all, the world's Christ? Where the spirit dwells, discords disappear and the life shines like the sun.

Where there is unity of spirit, there will gradually grow something like unity of form. Just what that will be we may not predict, but it will be such a spiritual organism as will allow the very life of God, as it was revealed in Jesus Christ, to reach and influence all races and all individuals without hindrance from human selfishness or prejudice. Enough for us to know now that the unity of the spirit will surely result in a growing unity of organization; and the more pervasive the spirit, the more perfect will be the form.

The unity of the spirit is a world-wide necessity. Those who exalt divisions belittle Christ. He is a sublime spiritual unity; the world needs him, — not some poor and puny fraction of his glorious body dissevered by those who do not understand him. There is money enough, and there are men enough, to send the gospel into every land, every home, every heart, and there it will be sent when the spirit of Christ is the inspiration of every movement which bears his name. What our time most needs is not a stronger organization, nor even simpler creeds, but Christian men who dare to be true to their inmost convictions; who are not afraid to fellowship with Jesus Christ wherever and in whomever they find him; who will have nothing to do with traditions or rules which interfere with the direct and constant leadership of his spirit, and who, appreciating all that it means, have said: "I will follow thee whithersoever thou goest." Such men will be misunderstood, and probably ostracized, but in them is the kingdom of God; and as their number increases, that unity of the spirit which is a world-wide necessity will become a reality as silently and beautifully as the springtime succeeds the winter.

www.ingramcontent.com/pod-product-compliance
Lightning Source LLC
Chambersburg PA
CBHW031749230426
43669CB00007B/556